FaithSharing for Teens

For
Barbara and Roy Theisen
March 2, 1957 to March 2, 2007

Celebrating 50 years of commitment
. . . in good times and bad
. . . in sickness and health
anchored by faith

Thanks, Mom and Dad,
for the model you are to all of us.

FaithSharing for Teens

25 Experiences that Connect Faith and Life

Michael Theisen

saint mary's press

The publishing team included Maura Thompson Hagarty, development editor; Lorraine Kilmartin, reviewer; Mary Koehler, permissions editor; prepress and manufacturing coordinated by the prepublication and production services departments of Saint Mary's Press.

Acknowledgments

The quotations on pages 88 and 89 are taken from the GodSpeaks: Simple, Relevant, Life-Changing Web site, *www.godspeaks.com/index/index.asp,* accessed April 20, 2006. Copyright © 2005 by GodSpeaks, Inc. Used with permission.

To view copyright terms and conditions for Internet materials cited here, log on to the home pages for the referenced Web sites.

During this book's preparation, all citations, facts, figures, names, addresses, telephone numbers, Internet URLs, and other pieces of information cited within were verified for accuracy. The authors and Saint Mary's Press staff have made every attempt to list current and valid sources, but we cannot guarantee the content of any source and we are not responsible for any changes that may have occurred since our verification. If you find an error in, or have a question or concern about, any of the information or sources listed within, please contact Saint Mary's Press.

Printed in the United States of America

3829

ISBN 978-0-88489-946-4

Library of Congress Cataloging-in-Publication Data

Theisen, Michael.
    FaithSharing for teens : 25 experiences that connect faith and life / Michael Theisen.
    p. cm.
ISBN 978-0-88489-946-4 (pbk.)
    1. Church group work with teenagers. 2. Teenagers—Religious life. 3. Small groups.
I. Title. II. Title: Faith sharing for teens.

BV4447.T44 2007
259'.23—dc22

                                                                    2006021926

Photo and Image Credits

Paul Casper: part three chapter openers, pages 75, 82, 104, and 112
FaithClipart: part one chapter openers, page 104
Juniperimages/Dynamicgraphics: pages 87 and 112
Clickart Incredible Image Pak: Parts Two and Four Chapter Openers, pages 97 and 112
Artville: page 108
Photodisc: pages 108 and 112
Tinka Sloss: page 104

Contents

Introduction

Faith Sharing: Connecting Faith with Life

Faith sharing is a relatively simple, yet profound, experience of seeking out the presence of God in the world and in our daily lives and sharing our discoveries with others. The more we are able to locate the intersection of our lives with the presence of God, the wider our eyes will open to see the active grace of God at work throughout our life journey.

Because God's presence cannot be defined or expressed by mere words, faith sharing often uses a metaphor, visual image, or other stimulation, such as music or guided meditation. This allows the participant to go beyond words in order to enter into and express this deeper level of connection with the ultimate mystery that is God.

Adolescents are at an opportune age to be introduced to faith sharing because of their increased ability to think metaphorically and symbolically. With the emergence of symbolic thought, teens become fascinated by the many levels of complex meaning ascribed to ordinary words and images. At this stage of intellectual development, it becomes natural for young people to get caught up in a higher level of reflection about life's ultimate questions, which inescapably leads them to wonder about the presence of God in the world.

Teenagers are also entering a period of "searching faith," where they begin to struggle with big questions about God, church, faith, and life. This searching is actually a positive movement, although it may appear on the outside to be anti-institutional, rebellious, and negative because of the amount of questioning and complaining often exhibited. The period of searching faith is an excellent time to introduce faith-sharing techniques and experiences because they are designed to encourage searching and questioning. Those who minister to and with young people can seize the opportunities presented by this moment of growth by introducing creative faith-sharing techniques that will challenge young people to step back and look for signs of God in their day-to-day lives.

The relational aspect of faith sharing is another reason why it is successful with young people. During the process, faith is shared with others. It is during this time of dialogue and connection that young people not only discover the meaning behind their own faith journey but also expand their insights simply by hearing about other people's journeys of faith. The more we can help young people to recognize that God is always with them, the more open they will be to looking for God's active hand at work in the world and in their lives.

The More We Look, the More We See

The faith-sharing process is a simple one: step back, reflect, and share. The various strategies used in *FaithSharing* all build upon this simple, yet profound, process. In fact, it behooves us as leaders to not complicate this process. We can show young people that faith sharing is not "rocket science" and that it can often be done in a relatively short amount of time, anywhere and at any time. Through frequent use of faith-sharing practices during gathered ministry times, young people can break open the Word of life within their ordinary surroundings.

The Content of *FaithSharing*

FaithSharing offers four different but related approaches to encourage young people to share their faith. Each approach uses a different focal point for faith sharing:

- Part 1: Scripture
- Part 2: Guided Meditation
- Part 3: Media Messages
- Part 4: Objects and Images

The experiences in each of the four parts use the simple process of stepping back, reflecting, and sharing.

The faith sharing with Scripture experiences in part 1 use a process adapted from *lectio divina*, an ancient monastic process of reflecting on a reading from Scripture or others' spiritual writings. The ten faith-sharing experiences in part 1 invite participants to reflect on a Scripture passage. They hear it three times, each time taking the meaning to a deeper level, and gradually open themselves up to allowing God to speak to and through them to others in the group. After completing these experiences, the participants and leaders will be familiar with the faith-sharing process. Additional experiences can be crafted by selecting a short Scripture passage and developing a question to help facilitate the reflection and the small-group sharing.

The five guided meditations in part 2 help take the listeners on a journey of faith in which they encounter the hand of God at work in their lives. Young people love guided meditations, mostly because meditation allows them time to do something they do not normally get to do: remain quiet and still. Within this stillness the listeners are led on a journey to face the issues and questions that are occupying their minds in the present moment. And when God is brought into this mix of concerns, the listeners are brought to a new level of insight and possibility.

The experiences in part 3 use objects and images to help young people share faith. An object or image is introduced to focus the group, so that people can begin to think symbolically and metaphorically about who God is, how God is present in their daily journey, and what God may be asking of them at the present time in their lives.

The experiences in part 4 use media messages. The participants focus on a form of media (song, magazine, billboard, movie, or TV show) as a starting point for making connections between life and faith.

There are twenty-five faith-sharing experiences in *FaithSharing*, and each one focuses young people on the presence of God in the here and now. The users of *FaithSharing* are encouraged to create more experiences that use its engaging strategies to lead young people to a deeper awareness of God in their lives.

Considerations for Faith Sharing

Group Size

Group size is an important factor for effective faith sharing. If a group is larger than ten people, divide it into small groups of five to seven people. If the group meets together on a regular basis, try to use the same groupings as much as possible so that a sense of trust and familiarity is developed. This will enhance the faith-sharing process over time.

Where and When to Use *FaithSharing*

Each experience in this resource can be carried out in 15 to 20 minutes, so the experiences are perfect for incorporation into retreats, youth gatherings, religious education sessions, lock-ins, and campus ministry settings. To get the most out of these faith-sharing experiences, it is best to use them when distractions are at a minimum. If young people are involved in a class or another type of learning session, the transition to faith sharing will work best at the end of the session rather than the beginning. If faith sharing is used in a retreat or another day-long or overnight event, evening is a better time to facilitate this process than earlier in the day. In short, the more time young people spend together, the more effective faith sharing will be for that group.

Not Teaching Time

Faith sharing is not a time for teaching, at least not in the formal sense. Faith sharing is a time for reflection and dialogue, a chance for young people to seek out the presence of God within their daily struggles and joys. Ideally, the teacher or leader serves as the facilitator of a journey during faith sharing and should be very careful not to impose a teaching methodology in the sense that a particular learning outcome is sought. Instead, leaders should mentally step out of the teaching role before beginning to lead a faith-sharing process. In fact, if *FaithSharing* is used in a classroom or school setting, which is strongly encouraged, have the students sit on the floor or actually move to another area of the room, so that the physical transition can serve as a ready reminder of the transition that is about to take place. This movement will also serve as a reminder to the leader to stop teaching and start facilitating faith sharing.

The leader, however, does not step out of his or her role as adult guide or mentor. He or she should be prepared to respond to comments that offend others or that inaccurately portray Catholic beliefs by reminding everyone to be respectful of others or by clarifying Church teaching.

Using the Mutual Invitation Process to Share Faith

Mutual invitation is a widely used process that allows everyone in the group to be empowered to share as well as to invite others to share. One person shares her or his reflection and then invites someone else in the group to share. The person just invited has the chance to share or pass. No matter what the person chooses to do, it is her or his responsibility to select the next person to share. The cycle continues until the last person shares and then re-invites those that passed the first time to share if they wish. It is important that this be done in a way that respects people's preferences not to share by allowing them to limit their sharing gracefully.

The reason mutual invitation works is that it essentially levels the playing field by avoiding "favorites" and giving everyone, not just the extroverts or natural leaders, the power both to share and to choose who shares next. This sharing of responsibility is an empowering experience for the whole group, and, once used, will likely become a sharing process of choice for many other group discussions.

Involving Youth

Research consistently indicates that the more the learner is involved in the learning process, the more he or she retains. The more we ask the question "How can the young people be more involved in this?" the more successful any event, strategy, or sharing experience will be. The same can be said for the process of faith sharing. The more we empower the young people to lead these experiences, the more these occasions will become opportunities for reflection and faith growth.

As Faith-Sharing Leaders

Once the designated leader begins to model the style and flow of the faith-sharing experiences in this book, the leader should begin empowering young people to take over the leadership (and selection) of the experiences. Empowering youth does not equal "dumping" responsibility on them without any training. Be sure the youth leader is prepared to lead the faith-sharing session by having her or him rehearse the process ahead of time, especially in the case of reading the guided meditations. The sooner the young people are given the support to lead faith sharing, the quicker they will begin to take responsibility for their own journeys of faith.

As Readers

Young people should be invited to proclaim the Scripture readings found in the faith-sharing experiences. With the process adapted from *lectio divina* in part 1, it is recommended that three different young people serve as readers. Having different voices proclaim the same reading may help lend new meaning to it. The readers should rehearse, so that their reading is truly a proclamation of Scripture and not just an experience of "reading out loud."

As Small-Group Prayer Leaders

Because faith sharing works best when one person initiates the sharing process, each small group should have a designated "prayer leader." The prayer leader's primary role is to begin when it is time to share and to encourage the small-group members to remain focused and reverent during the process. They may also help with distributing supplies and finding Scripture passages.

A Final Word

Ownership—that is what users of *FaithSharing* want to strive for: inspiring every young person to take ownership of their own faith. The leader's goal is to help the young people embrace their faith and their journey and to help them come to know that God is a part of it all. The more we can lead teenagers toward owning their faith, the more active, involved, and faith-filled will be the people within our Church and the world. And that is good news for us all!

Part One

Faith Sharing with Scripture

What Is Faith Sharing with Scripture?

This approach to faith sharing is an adaptation of *lectio divina*, meaning "divine or prayful reading." *Lectio divina* refers to a method of reflection on spiritual writings, most often Scripture, that originated centuries ago in monastic communities. Individuals read or listen to a proclamation of a passage several times and meditate on words or phrases that strike them as significant. The goal of this process is to hear God speaking through the passage and to respond in prayer. The repetition of the same passage is intended to help the participants listen attentively with open hearts and minds and discover the meaning of the passage and its significance for their lives. The process engages the mind, but it is much more than an intellectual exercise. It is meant to foster a conversation between the participant and God.

The Adapted Process

FaithSharing introduces adolescents to a short process for faith sharing with Scripture in small groups. Each of the ten experiences included in part 1 of this resource invites the participants to prayerfully meditate on a selected Scripture passage.

The leader introduces each faith-sharing experience in this section with a few moments of centered breathing and then says a short prayer to help focus the participants on the word of God. Then he or she provides a brief introduction to the Scripture passage, which is read three times. The leader guides a process of reflection and sharing for each reading, each time with a different focus:

- Reading One: reflection on *one word*
- Reading Two: reflection on *one phrase*
- Reading Three: reflection on *what God is saying* through the reading

Once the process has been used several times, leaders and young people will quickly develop a proficiency in using this faith-sharing approach with any Scripture passage, in either personal or group prayer.

Scripture 1
Anger

Scripture: Ephesians 4:25–26,29–32

Overview

Anger, gossip, and bitterness often have their roots in fear and can easily get the better of us if we allow it. This reading from Paul's Letter to the Ephesians will challenge the participants to reflect on how God is calling them to speak the truth with compassion and without fear, anger, or bitterness ruling their hearts.

Estimated Time: 15–20 minutes

Preparation Steps

- Gather the following items:
  - ☐ paper and a pen or pencil for each participant
  - ☐ copies of *The Catholic Youth Bible*® or another Bible, one for each participant (optional)
- Mark the Scripture reading (Ephesians 4:25–26,29–32) in a Bible.
- Select one or more readers to proclaim the three readings.

Procedure

Step 1: Overview of Process and Creation of Faith-Sharing Groups

Introduce the faith sharing with Scripture process using these or similar words:

- ○ This faith-sharing experience is adapted from an ancient Catholic prayer style called *lectio divina,* or "divine reading." This prayerful reading invites us to open ourselves up to Scripture so that God may speak to us as well as through us to others around us.

14

o The process follows a simple formula. We will listen to the proclamation of a short Scripture passage three times. I will suggest a focus for your reflection during each reading. After each you will be invited to share some thoughts that came to mind during the reading. When it is your turn, please say "pass" if you do not wish to share.

If the group size is larger than ten, divide into small faith-sharing groups of five to seven. Select one person in each faith-sharing group to serve as a prayer leader.

Distribute paper and pens or pencils to each participant. If you are providing participants with bibles, distribute those also.

Step 2: Introduction and Reading One

Introduce this faith-sharing experience by inviting the participants to quiet themselves and focus on their breathing. Ask them to spend a full 30 seconds simply listening to their breathing, and then offer the following introductory prayer:

o Word of God, gift us with ears to hear your words and hearts that will seek your wisdom.

Proceed with the comments below:

o Listen closely to this reading from Paul's letter to the Ephesians. He writes about what to do with anger and bitterness. As you listen, think about how anger has affected you this week and open yourself to the one word that God is trying to speak to you today. Please select only one word. When the reading is finished, each of you will be invited to share your word with your small group.

Invite the designated reader to proclaim Ephesians 4:25–26,29–32 slowly and prayerfully to the group.

Step 3: Sharing One Word

Invite the participants to share the one word they selected during the reading with the members of their small group. Ask the prayer leader in each group to begin. Remind everyone to share just the one word.

Step 4: Reading Two

Prepare everyone for the second reading using these or similar words:

o During the second proclamation of the passage, listen for the phrase or sentence that God is trying to speak to you today. It does not have to contain the word that you just shared. When the reading is finished, each of you will have an opportunity to share that phrase with your small group.

Invite the designated reader to proclaim Ephesians 4:25–26,29–32 slowly and prayerfully to the group.

Step 5: Sharing the Phrase

Invite each small-group prayer leader to share her or his phrase and then give everyone else in the small group an opportunity to share their phrases. Remind everyone to share just the phrase, without further explanation.

Step 6: Reading Three

Prepare everyone for the third reading using these or similar words:
- Listen to the reading one last time. Open yourself up to how God is asking you to apply this reading to your life today. When the reading is finished, you will have some time to reflect on what God is saying to you and to share your reflection with your group if you wish.

Invite the designated reader to proclaim Ephesians 4:25–26,29–32 slowly and prayerfully to the group.

Step 7: Sharing the Reflection

Explain to the participants that they will now have a short period of silence to reflect on what God is saying to them. Invite them to use the paper to write thoughts or draw images that come to mind during the reflection period. After a minute or two of quiet reflection, invite the participants to begin sharing their reflections in their small groups using the mutual invitation process.

Note: If the participants are unfamiliar with this process, take a minute to summarize the description on page 10 (see "Using the Mutual Invitation Process to Share Faith" in the introduction). Be sure to remind them of the option to pass.

Allow several minutes for this sharing.

Step 8: Conclusion and Closing Prayer

Conclude with these or similar words:
- Whether you experienced God's response clearly, somewhat, or not at all, it does not take away from the fact that God has been present to and through us during this time, speaking to us through our thoughts, through our consciences, and through those around us about anger, bitterness, and forgiveness.

- As we conclude this time together, let us take to heart what we have heard from within and from one another during this time of faith sharing and allow it to challenge us to live as disciples today and in the week to come.

Close by inviting everyone to join hands and slowly pray the Lord's Prayer together.

Scripture 2
Anxiety and Stress

Scripture: Matthew 6:25–30

Overview

Anxiety, stress, and worry are big obstacles for young people today. Many times, these problems arise when young people allow their thoughts to be overtaken by fears of "what if?" and laments over what has occurred in the past. This faith-sharing experience invites young people to center themselves on the well-known "lilies of the fields" passage from the Gospel of Matthew in order to discover God's presence in their midst.

Estimated Time: 15–20 minutes

Preparation Steps

- Gather the following items:
  - ☐ paper and a pen or pencil for each participant
  - ☐ copies of THE CATHOLIC YOUTH BIBLE or another Bible, one for each participant (optional)
- Mark the Scripture reading (Matthew 6:25–30) in a Bible.
- Select one or more readers to proclaim the three readings.

Procedure

Step 1: Overview of Process and Creation of Faith-Sharing Groups

Introduce the faith sharing with Scripture process using these or similar words:

○ This faith-sharing experience is adapted from an ancient Catholic prayer style called *lectio divina,* or "divine reading." This prayerful reading invites us to open ourselves up to Scripture so that God may speak to us as well as through us to others around us.

○ The process follows a simple formula. We will listen to the proclamation of a short Scripture passage three times. I will suggest a focus for your reflection during each reading. After each you will be invited to share some thoughts that came to mind during the reading. When it is your turn, please say "pass" if you do not wish to share.

If the group size is larger than ten, divide into small faith-sharing groups of five to seven. Select one person in each faith-sharing group to serve as a prayer leader.

Distribute paper and pens or pencils to each participant. If you are providing participants with bibles, distribute those also.

Step 2: Introduction and Reading One

Introduce this faith-sharing experience by inviting the participants to quiet themselves and focus on their breathing. Ask them to spend a full 30 seconds simply listening to their breathing, and then offer the following introductory prayer:

○ Word of God, unclutter our minds and free our thoughts so that we may spend this moment with you.

Proceed with the comments below:

○ Listen intently to this reading from Matthew's Gospel as Jesus speaks to the crowd about worries and concerns. As you listen to it, place yourself in the crowd that Jesus is talking to and open yourself up to the one word that God is trying to speak to you today. Please select only one word. When the reading is finished, each of you will be invited to share the word in your group.

Invite the designated readers to proclaim Matthew 6:25–30 slowly and prayerfully to the group.

Step 3: Sharing One Word

Invite the participants to share the one word they selected during the reading with the members of their small group. Ask the prayer leader in each group to begin. Remind everyone to share just the one word.

Step 4: Reading Two

Prepare everyone for the second reading using these or similar words:

○ During the second proclamation of the passage, listen for the phrase or sentence that God is trying to speak to you today. It does not have to contain the word that you just shared. When the reading is finished, each of you will have an opportunity to share that phrase with your small group.

Invite the designated reader to proclaim Matthew 6:25–30 slowly and prayerfully to the group.

Step 5: Sharing the Phrase

Invite each small-group prayer leader to share his or her phrase, and then give everyone else in the small group an opportunity to share their phrases. Remind everyone to share just the phrase, without further explanation.

Step 6: Reading Three

○ Listen to the reading one last time. Open yourself up to how God is asking you to apply this reading to your life today. When the reading is finished, you will have some time to reflect on what God is saying to you and to share your reflection with your group if you wish.

Invite the designated reader to proclaim Matthew 6:25–30 slowly and prayerfully to the group.

Step 7: Sharing the Reflection

Explain to the participants that they will now have a short period of silence to reflect on what God is saying to them. Invite them to use the paper to write thoughts or draw images that come to mind during the reflection period. After a minute or two of quiet reflection, invite the participants to begin sharing their reflections in their small groups using the mutual invitation process.

Note: If the participants are unfamiliar with this process, take a minute to summarize the description on page 10 (see "Using the Mutual Invitation Process to Share Faith" in the introduction). Be sure to remind them of the option to pass.

Allow several minutes for this sharing.

Step 8: Conclusion and Closing Prayer

Conclude with these or similar words:
○ During this faith-sharing experience, God has been speaking to you through the Scripture readings, your reflections, and your small-group sharing. Let us take to heart what we have heard about stress, anxiety, and worry. Let it challenge us to live each day as a gift from God to be opened and lived to the fullest.

Close by inviting everyone to join hands and slowly pray the Lord's Prayer together.

Scripture 3
Hope

Scripture: Romans 8:18–25

Overview

This faith-sharing experience uses a passage from Romans to address the theme of hope—what it is and what it is not. During the process, the young people are invited to reflect on the hope they yearn for now and in the week to come.

Estimated Time: 15–20 minutes

Preparation Steps

- Gather the following items:
  - ☐ paper and a pen or pencil for each participant
  - ☐ copies of THE CATHOLIC YOUTH BIBLE or another Bible, one for each participant (optional)
- Mark the Scripture reading (Romans 8:18–25) in a Bible.
- Select one or more readers to proclaim the three readings.

Procedure

Step 1: Overview of Process and Creation of Faith-Sharing Groups

Introduce the faith sharing with Scripture process using these or similar words:

- ○ This faith-sharing experience is adapted from an ancient Catholic prayer style called *lectio divina,* or "divine reading." This prayerful reading invites us to open ourselves up to Scripture so that God may speak to us as well as through us to others around us.

○ The process follows a simple formula. We will listen to the proclamation of a short Scripture passage three times. I will suggest a focus for your reflection during each reading. After each you will be invited to share some thoughts that came to mind during the reading. When it is your turn, please say "pass" if you do not wish to share.

If the group size is larger than ten, divide into small faith-sharing groups of five to seven. Select one person in each faith-sharing group to serve as a prayer leader.

Distribute paper and pens or pencils to each participant. If you are providing participants with bibles, distribute those also.

Step 2: Introduction and Reading One

Introduce this faith-sharing experience by inviting the participants to quiet themselves and focus on their breathing. Ask them to spend a full 30 seconds simply listening to their breathing, and then offer the following introductory prayer:

○ Word of God, gift us with ears to hear your words and hearts that will seek your wisdom.

Proceed with the comments below:

○ Listen closely to this reading from Paul's Letter to the Romans. He writes about the power and promise of hope. As you listen, think about what has given you hope or taken it away this past week, and open yourself to the one word that God is trying to speak to you today. Please select only one word. When the reading is finished, each of you will be invited to share your word with your small group.

Invite the designated reader to proclaim Romans 8:18–25 slowly and prayerfully to the group.

Step 3: Sharing One Word

Invite the participants to share the one word they selected during the reading with the members of their small group. Ask the prayer leader in each group to begin. Remind everyone to share just the one word.

Step 4: Reading Two

Prepare everyone for the second reading using these or similar words:

○ During the second proclamation of the passage, listen for the phrase or sentence that God is trying to speak to you today. It does not have to contain the word that you just shared. When the reading is finished, each of you will have an opportunity to share that phrase with your small group.

Invite the designated reader to proclaim Romans 8:18–25 slowly and prayerfully to the group.

Step 5: Sharing the Phrase

Invite each small-group prayer leader to share her or his phrase and then give everyone else in the small group an opportunity to share their phrases. Remind everyone to share just the phrase, without further explanation.

Step 6: Reading Three

Prepare everyone for the third reading using these or similar words:

○ Listen to the reading one last time. Open yourself up to how God is asking you to apply this reading to your life today. When the reading is finished, you will have some time to reflect on what God is saying to you and to share your reflection with your group if you wish.

Invite the designated reader to proclaim Romans 8:18–25 slowly and prayerfully to the group.

Step 7: Sharing the Reflection

Explain to the participants that they will now have a short period of silence to reflect on what God is saying to them. Invite them to use the paper to write thoughts or draw images that come to mind during the reflection period. After a minute or two of quiet reflection, invite the participants to begin sharing their reflections in their small groups using the mutual invitation process.

Note: If the participants are unfamiliar with this process, take a minute to summarize the description on page 10 (see "Using the Mutual Invitation Process to Share Faith" in the introduction). Be sure to remind them of the option to pass.

Allow several minutes for this sharing.

Step 8: Conclusion and Closing Prayer

Conclude with these or similar words:

○ Through our sharing, God has been speaking to and through us about the theme of hope. As you reflect on what has been shared, focus on the hope in your life right now or your desire for greater hope, especially this coming week, and consider offering this to God in prayer now.

Lead a brief final prayer by inviting the participants to share one hope they have for the coming week. Ask the group to respond to each hope with "Lord of hope, hear our prayer." Begin the prayer with these or similar words:

○ Lord of all hopefulness, you have been present to us in our sharing. Now we ask you to be present to us as we bring to you our hope-filled petitions.

Close by inviting the participants to pray the Lord's Prayer together.

Scripture 4
God's Presence

Scripture: Psalm 138

Overview

It is not unusual at times to wonder where God is. Thousands of years ago a psalmist wondered the same thing. This faith-sharing experience invites the participants to reflect on Psalm 138, a joyful hymn of thanksgiving that celebrates the discovery that God is always present and loving and will never abandon or forsake us.

Estimated Time: 15–20 minutes

Preparation Steps

- Gather the following items:
  - ☐ paper and a pen or pencil for each participant
  - ☐ copies of THE CATHOLIC YOUTH BIBLE or another Bible, one for each participant (optional)
- Mark the Scripture reading (Psalm 138) in a Bible.
- Select one or more readers to proclaim the three readings.

Procedure

Step 1: Overview of Process and Creation of Faith-Sharing Groups

Introduce the faith sharing with Scripture process using these or similar words:

- ○ This faith-sharing experience is adapted from an ancient Catholic prayer style called *lectio divina,* or "divine reading." This prayerful

reading invites us to open ourselves up to Scripture so that God may speak to us as well as through us to others around us.

o The process follows a simple formula. We will listen to the proclamation of a short Scripture passage three times. I will suggest a focus for your reflection during each reading. After each you will be invited to share some thoughts that came to mind during the reading. When it is your turn, please say "pass" if you do not wish to share.

If the group size is larger than ten, divide into small faith-sharing groups of five to seven. Select one person in each faith-sharing group to serve as a prayer leader.

Distribute paper and pens or pencils to each participant. If you are providing participants with bibles, distribute those also.

Step 2: Introduction and Reading One

Introduce this faith-sharing experience by inviting the participants to quiet themselves and focus on their breathing. Ask them to spend a full 30 seconds simply listening to their breathing, and then offer the following introductory prayer:

o Word of God, gift us with ears to hear your words and hearts that will seek your wisdom.

Proceed with the comments below:

o Listen closely to this reading from the Book of Psalms, which highlights God's active presence and responsive faithfulness to those who believe in him. As you listen, think about how you encountered God's presence this past week and open yourself to the one word that God is trying to speak to you today. Please select only one word. When the reading is finished, each of you will be invited to share your word with your small group.

Invite the designated reader to proclaim Psalm 138 slowly and prayerfully to the group.

Step 3: Sharing One Word

Invite the participants to share the one word they selected during the reading with the members of their small group. Ask the prayer leader in each group to begin. Remind everyone to share just the one word.

Step 4: Reading Two

Prepare everyone for the second reading using these or similar words:

o During the second proclamation of the passage, listen for the phrase or sentence that God is trying to speak to you today. It does not have to contain the word that you just shared. When the reading is finished,

each of you will have an opportunity to share that phrase with your small group.

Invite the designated reader to proclaim Psalm 138 slowly and prayerfully to the group.

Step 5: Sharing the Phrase

Invite each small-group prayer leader to share his or her phrase, and then give everyone else in the small group an opportunity to share their phrases. Remind everyone to share just the phrase, without further explanation.

Step 6: Reading Three

Prepare everyone for the third reading using these or similar words:
  ○ Listen to the reading one last time. Open yourself up to how God is asking you to apply this reading to your life today. When the reading is finished, you will have some time to reflect on what God is saying to you and to share your reflection with your group if you wish.

Invite the designated reader to proclaim Psalm 138 slowly and prayerfully to the group.

Step 7: Sharing the Reflection

Explain to the participants that they have a short period of silence now to reflect on what God is saying to them. Invite them to use the paper to write thoughts or draw images that come to mind during the reflection period. After a minute or two of quiet reflection, invite the participants to begin sharing their reflections in their small groups, using the mutual invitation process.

Note: If the participants are unfamiliar with this process, take a minute to summarize the description on page 10 (see "Using the Mutual Invitation Process to Share Faith" in the introduction). Be sure to remind them of the option to pass.

Allow several minutes for this sharing.

Step 8: Conclusion and Closing Prayer

Conclude with these or similar words:
  ○ It is not unusual at times to wonder where God is. Sometimes this thought is prompted by wonder, sometimes by anger, and sometimes by loss. When we ask where God is in prayer, we are likely to discover the hand of God at work within and through us if we listen attentively for a reply.

- As you reflect on the presence of God in your life this past week, consider what prayer of thanksgiving you wish to offer to God.

Lead the participants in a final prayer by inviting everyone to think about what God has done for them this past week. Then complete aloud the sentence, "Thank you, God, for . . ." Close by inviting everyone to pray the Lord's Prayer together.

Scripture 5
Love

Scripture: 1 Corinthians 13:1–8a

Overview

This faith-sharing experience invites young people to see love as an essential ingredient in life, one that gives our lives meaning, heals us, challenges us, and motivates us. Using Paul's first letter to the Church of Corinth, the young people are invited to reflect on how God is calling each of them to love one another.

Estimated Time: 15–20 minutes

Preparation Steps

* Gather the following items:
    - [ ] paper and a pen or pencil for each participant

    - [ ] copes of THE CATHOLIC YOUTH BIBLE or another Bible, one for each participant (optional)

* Mark the Scripture reading (1 Corinthians 13:1–8a) in a Bible.
* Select one or more readers to proclaim the three readings.

Procedure

Step 1: Overview of Process and Creation of Faith-Sharing Groups

Introduce the faith sharing with Scripture process using these or similar words:

   ○ This faith-sharing experience is adapted from an ancient Catholic prayer style called *lectio divina,* or "divine reading." This prayerful

reading invites us to open ourselves up to Scripture so that God may speak to us as well as through us to others around us.

○ The process follows a simple formula. We will listen to the proclamation of a short Scripture passage three times. I will suggest a focus for your reflection during each reading. After each you will be invited to share some thoughts that came to mind during the reading. When it is your turn, please say "pass" if you do not wish to share.

If the group size is larger than ten, divide into small faith-sharing groups of five to seven. Select one person in each faith-sharing group to serve as a prayer leader.

Distribute paper and pens or pencils to each participant. If you are providing participants with bibles, distribute those also.

Step 2: Introduction and Reading One

Introduce this faith-sharing experience by inviting the participants to quiet themselves and focus on their breathing. Ask them to spend a full 30 seconds simply listening to their breathing, and then offer the following introductory prayer:

○ Word of God, gift us with ears to hear your words and hearts that will seek your wisdom.

Proceed with the comments below:

○ Listen closely to this reading from Paul's First Letter to the Corinthians. He writes about what love is and what it is not. As you listen, reflect on the kind of love you have experienced this past week and open yourself to the one word that God is trying to speak to you today. Please select only one word. When the reading is finished, each of you will share your word with the group.

Invite the designated reader to proclaim 1 Corinthians 13:1–8a slowly and prayerfully to the group.

Step 3: Sharing One Word

Invite the participants to share the one word they selected during the reading with the members of their small group. Ask the prayer leader in each group to begin. Remind everyone to share just the one word.

Step 4: Reading Two

Prepare everyone for the second reading using these or similar words:

○ During the second proclamation of the passage, listen for the phrase or sentence that God is trying to speak to you today. It does not have to contain the word that you just shared. When the reading is finished,

each of you will have an opportunity to share that phrase with your small group.

Invite the designated reader to proclaim 1 Corinthians 13:1–8a slowly and prayerfully to the group.

Step 5: Sharing the Phrase

Invite each small-group prayer leader to share her or his phrase and then give everyone else in the small group an opportunity to share their phrases. Remind everyone to share just the phrase, without further explanation.

Step 6: Reading Three

Prepare everyone for the third reading using these or similar words:

○ Listen to the reading one last time. Open yourself up to how God is asking you to apply this reading to your life today. When the reading is finished, you will have some time to reflect on what God is saying to you and to share your reflection with your group if you wish.

Invite the designated reader to proclaim 1 Corinthians 13:1–8a slowly and prayerfully to the group.

Step 7: Sharing the Reflection

Explain to the participants that they will now have a short period of silence to reflect on what God is saying to them. Invite them to use the paper to write thoughts or draw images that come to mind during the reflection period. After a minute or two of quiet reflection, invite the participants to begin sharing their reflections in their small groups, using the mutual invitation process.

Note: If the participants are unfamiliar with this process, take a minute to summarize the description on page 10 (see "Using the Mutual Invitation Process to Share Faith" in the introduction). Be sure to remind them of the option to pass.

Allow several minutes for this sharing.

Step 8: Conclusion and Closing Prayer

Conclude with these or similar words:

○ God's love is revealed to us through those who take this reading to heart.

○ Think about what God has spoken to you today about love and where it is present or absent in your life right now.

Invite everyone to join hands and pray together the Lord's Prayer. Then close by inviting the participants to exchange a sign of peace with one another.

Scripture 6
Peace

Scripture: John 14:23–27

Overview

The Hebrew word *shalom* means "deep, lasting peace." In this reading from John's Gospel, Jesus says this word when he blesses his followers. This peace is a holy, God-given peace intended to help the disciples bear the hardships of faith. This faith-sharing experience invites the young people to consider the place of peace (*shalom*) in their lives and how "peace-full" they have felt this week.

Estimated Time: 15–20 minutes

Preparation Steps

- Gather the following items:
  - ☐ paper and a pen or pencil for each participant
  - ☐ copies of THE CATHOLIC YOUTH BIBLE or another Bible, one for each participant (optional)
  - ☐ copies of handout 6–A, "The Prayer of Saint Francis," one for each participant
- Mark the Scripture reading (John 14:23–27) in a Bible.
- Select one or more readers to proclaim the three readings.

Procedure

Step 1: Overview of Process and Creation of Faith-Sharing Groups

Introduce the faith sharing with Scripture process using these or similar words:

○ This faith-sharing experience is adapted from an ancient Catholic prayer style called *lectio divina,* or "divine reading." This prayerful reading invites us to open ourselves up to Scripture so that God may speak to us as well as through us to others around us.

○ The process follows a simple formula. We will listen to the proclamation of a short Scripture passage three times. I will suggest a focus for your reflection during each reading. After each you will be invited to share some thoughts that came to mind during the reading. When it is your turn, please say "pass" if you do not wish to share.

If the group size is larger than ten, divide into small faith-sharing groups of five to seven. Select one person in each faith-sharing group to serve as a prayer leader.

Distribute paper and pens or pencils to each participant. If you are providing participants with bibles, distribute those also.

Step 2: Introduction and Reading One

Introduce this faith-sharing experience by inviting the participants to quiet themselves and focus on their breathing. Ask them to spend a full 30 seconds simply listening to their breathing, and then offer the following introductory prayer:

○ Word of God, gift us with ears to hear your words and hearts that will seek your wisdom.

Proceed with the comments below:

○ Listen closely to this reading from the Gospel of John in which Jesus talks about a special kind of peace that is not of this world. As you listen, think about the place of peace in your life and how peaceful you have felt this week. Open yourself to the one word that God is trying to speak to you today. Please select only one word. When the reading is finished, each of you will be invited to share your word with your small group.

Invite the designated reader to proclaim John 14:23–27 slowly and prayerfully to the group.

Step 3: Sharing One Word

Invite the participants to share the one word they selected during the reading with the members of their small group. Ask the prayer leader in each group to begin. Remind everyone to share just the one word.

Step 4: Reading Two

Prepare everyone for the second reading using these or similar words:

○ During the second proclamation of the passage, listen for the phrase or sentence that God is trying to speak to you today. It does not have to contain the word that you just shared. When the reading is finished, each of you will have an opportunity to share that phrase with your small group.

Invite the designated reader to proclaim John 14:23–27 slowly and prayerfully to the group.

Step 5: Sharing the Phrase

Invite each small-group prayer leader to share his or her phrase, and then give everyone else in the small group an opportunity to share their phrases. Remind everyone to share just the phrase, without further explanation.

Step 6: Reading Three

Prepare everyone for the third reading using these or similar words:

○ Listen to the reading one last time. Open yourself up to how God is asking you to apply this reading to your life today. When the reading is finished, you will have some time to reflect on what God is saying to you and to share your reflection with your group if you wish.

Invite the designated reader to proclaim John 14:23–27 slowly and prayerfully to the group.

Step 7: Sharing the Reflection

Explain to the participants that they will now have a short period of silence to reflect on what God is saying to them. Invite them to use the paper to write thoughts or draw images that come to mind during the reflection period. After a minute or two of quiet reflection, invite the participants to begin sharing their reflections in their small groups using the mutual invitation process.

Note: If the participants are unfamiliar with this process, take a minute to summarize the description on page 10 (see "Using the Mutual Invitation Process to Share Faith" in the introduction). Be sure to remind them of the option to pass.

Allow several minutes for this sharing.

Step 8: Conclusion and Closing Prayer

Conclude with these or similar words:

○ God has been made present today through our sharing.

○ Think about the peace that is needed to fill our hearts and our world.

Distribute handout 6–A, "The Prayer of Saint Francis," and invite everyone to pray the prayer together.

Close by inviting everyone to exchange a sign of peace.

The Prayer of Saint Francis

Lord, make me an instrument of your peace;

where there is hatred, let me sow love;

where there is injury, pardon;

where there is doubt, faith;

where there is despair, hope;

where there is darkness, light;

where there is sadness, joy.

Grant that I may not so much seek

to be consoled as to console,

to be understood as to understand,

to be loved as to love;

for it is in giving that we receive,

it is in pardoning that we are pardoned,

and it is in dying that we are born to eternal life.

Amen.

Scripture 7
Friendship

Scripture: Sirach 6:5–17

Overview

This faith-sharing experience invites young people to reflect on friendship. They will hear a reading from Sirach about the characteristics that a true friend possesses. The participants will consider who their true friends are and the nature of the friendship that participants offer to others.

Estimated Time: 15–20 minutes

Preparation Steps

- Gather the following items:
  - ☐ paper and a pen or pencil for each participant
  - ☐ copies of THE CATHOLIC YOUTH BIBLE or another Bible, one for each participant (optional)
- Mark the Scripture reading (Sirach 6:5–17) in a Bible.
- Select one or more readers to proclaim the three readings.

Procedure

Step 1: Overview of Process and Creation of Faith-Sharing Groups

Introduce the faith sharing with Scripture process using these or similar words:

  - ○ This faith-sharing experience is adapted from an ancient Catholic prayer style called *lectio divina,* or "divine reading." This prayerful

reading invites us to open ourselves up to Scripture so that God may speak to us as well as through us to others around us.

- The process follows a simple formula. We will listen to the proclamation of a short Scripture passage three times. I will suggest a focus for your reflection during each reading. After each you will be invited to share some thoughts that came to mind during the reading. When it is your turn, please say "pass" if you do not wish to share.

If the group size is larger than ten, divide into small faith-sharing groups of five to seven. Select one person in each faith-sharing group to serve as a prayer leader.

Distribute paper and pens or pencils to each participant. If you are providing participants with bibles, distribute those also.

Step 2: Introduction and Reading Two

Introduce this faith-sharing experience by inviting the participants to quiet themselves and focus on their breathing. Ask them to spend a full 30 seconds simply listening to their breathing, and then offer the following introductory prayer:

- Word of God, gift us with ears to hear your words and hearts that will seek your wisdom.

Proceed with the comments below:

- Listen closely to this reading from the Old Testament Book of Sirach about what true friendship is and what it is not. As you listen, reflect on the meaning of friendship in your life, especially this past week, and open yourself to the one word that God is trying to speak to you today about friendship. Please select only one word. When the reading is finished, each of you will be invited to share your word with your small group.

Invite the designated reader to proclaim Sirach 6:5–17 slowly and prayerfully to the group.

Step 3: Sharing One Word

Invite the participants to share the one word they selected during the reading with the members of their small group. Ask the prayer leader in each group to begin. Remind everyone to share just the one word.

Step 4: Reading Two

Prepare everyone for the second reading using these or similar words:

- During the second proclamation of the passage, listen for the phrase or sentence that God is trying to speak to you today. It does not have to contain the word that you just shared. When the reading is finished,

each of you will have an opportunity to share that phrase with your small group.

Invite the designated reader to proclaim Sirach 6:5–17 slowly and prayerfully to the group.

Step 5: Sharing the Phrase

Invite each small-group prayer leader to share her or his phrase and then give everyone else in the small group an opportunity to share their phrases. Remind everyone to share just the phrase, without further explanation.

Step 6: Reading Three

Prepare everyone for the third reading using these or similar words:
- Listen to the reading one last time. Open yourself up to how God is asking you to apply this reading to your life today. When the reading is finished, you will have some time to reflect on what God is saying to you and to share your reflection with your group if you wish.

Invite the designated reader to proclaim Sirach 6:5–17 slowly and prayerfully to the group.

Step 7: Sharing the Reflection

Explain to the participants that they will now have a short period of silence to reflect on what God is saying to them. Invite them to use the paper to write thoughts or draw images that come to mind during the reflection period. After a minute or two of quiet reflection, invite the participants to begin sharing their reflections in their small groups, using the mutual invitation process.

Note: If the participants are unfamiliar with this process, take a minute to summarize the description on page 10 (see "Using the Mutual Invitation Process to Share Faith" in the introduction). Be sure to remind them of the option to pass.

Allow several minutes for this sharing.

Step 8: Conclusion and Closing Prayer

Conclude with these or similar words:
- To have a good friend, one must be a good friend, especially during the difficult times. Think of a person or persons who have taught you about true friendship. In a moment, you will be invited to share these persons' first names during our closing prayer.

Lead the following prayer:

○ Lord, you called those who followed you "friend" because you shared everything with them. Thank you for the gift of your friendship as well as the gift of those true friends who walk this journey of faith and life with us.

Please call out the first name(s) of the friend(s) that you wish to add to this prayer. (Pause for names to be said aloud.)

○ Lord, we ask your blessing upon all of these special people this day and especially in the coming weeks. We ask this prayer through Christ, our friend and our Savior. Amen.

Scripture 8
Justice

Scripture: Isaiah 11:1–9

Overview

This faith-sharing experience invites the participants to think about those who are poor and oppressed. The young people will consider God's call to act for justice and reflect on how their gifts can help those who are in need.

Estimated Time: 15–20 minutes

Preparation Steps

- Gather the following items:
  - ☐ paper and a pen or pencil for each participant
  - ☐ copies of THE CATHOLIC YOUTH BIBLE or another Bible, one for each participant (optional)
- Mark the Scripture reading (Isaiah 11:1–9) in a Bible.
- Select one or more readers to proclaim the three readings.

Procedure

Step 1: Overview of Process and Creation of Faith-Sharing Groups

Introduce the faith sharing with Scripture process using these or similar words:

- ○ This faith-sharing experience is adapted from an ancient Catholic prayer style called *lectio divina,* or "divine reading." This prayerful reading invites us to open ourselves up to Scripture so that God may speak to us as well as through us to others around us.

o The process follows a simple formula. We will listen to the proclamation of a short Scripture passage three times. I will suggest a focus for your reflection during each reading. After each you will be invited to share some thoughts that came to mind during the reading. When it is your turn, please say "pass" if you do not wish to share.

If the group size is larger than ten, divide into small faith-sharing groups of five to seven. Select one person in each faith-sharing group to serve as a prayer leader.

Distribute paper and pens or pencils to each participant. If you are providing participants with bibles, distribute those also.

Step 2: Introduction and Reading One

Introduce this faith-sharing experience by inviting the participants to quiet themselves and focus on their breathing. Ask them to spend a full 30 seconds simply listening to their breathing, and then offer the following introductory prayer:

o Word of God, gift us with ears to hear your words and hearts that will seek your wisdom.

Proceed with the comments below:

o Listen closely to this reading from the prophet Isaiah, who speaks about the coming of a Savior who will bring justice to the world. As you listen, think about oppressed people that you encounter every day, those with little power or influence. As you do so, think about the one word that God is trying to speak to you today. Please select only one word. When the reading is finished, each of you will be invited to share your word with your small group.

Invite the designated reader to proclaim Isaiah 11:1–9 slowly and prayerfully to the group.

Step 3: Sharing One Word

Invite the participants to share the one word they selected during the reading with the members of their small group. Ask the prayer leader in each group to begin. Remind everyone to share just the one word.

Step 4: Reading Two

Prepare everyone for the second reading using these or similar words:

o During the second proclamation of the passage, listen for the phrase or sentence that God is trying to speak to you today. It does not have to contain the word that you just shared. When the reading is finished, each of you will have an opportunity to share that phrase with your small group.

Invite the designated reader to proclaim Isaiah 11:1–9 slowly and prayerfully to the group.

Step 5: Sharing the Phrase

Invite each small-group prayer leader to share his or her phrase, and then give everyone else in the small group an opportunity to share their phrases. Remind everyone to share just the phrase, without further explanation.

Step 6: Reading Three

Prepare everyone for the third reading using these or similar words:
- Listen to the reading one last time. Open yourself up to how God is asking you to apply this reading to your life today. When the reading is finished, you will have some time to reflect on what God is saying to you and to share your reflection with your group if you wish.

Invite the designated reader to proclaim Isaiah 11:1–9 slowly and prayerfully to the group.

Step 7: Sharing the Reflection

Explain to the participants that they will now have a short period of silence to reflect on what God is saying to them. Invite them to use the paper to write thoughts or draw images that come to mind during the reflection period. After a minute or two of quiet reflection, invite the participants to begin sharing their reflections in their small groups using the mutual invitation process.

Note: If the participants are unfamiliar with this process, take a minute to summarize the description on page 10 (see "Using the Mutual Invitation Process to Share Faith" in the introduction). Be sure to remind them of the option to pass.

Allow several minutes for this sharing.

Step 8: Conclusion and Closing Prayer

Conclude with these or similar words:
- If we want to claim the title "Christian," we must accept responsibility for upholding justice.

- As we conclude, let us commit ourselves to responding to God's call to act with justice.

- Consider at least one way that you can say "Amen" (yes!) to this challenge during the coming week.

Close by inviting everyone to join hands and pray the Lord's Prayer together.

Scripture 9
Forgiveness

Scripture: Luke 6:36–42

Overview

This faith-sharing experience invites the young people to consider how God is calling out to each of them to embrace the gospel value of forgiveness.

Estimated Time: 15–20 minutes

Preparation Steps

- Gather the following items:
    - ☐ paper and a pen or pencil for each participant
    - ☐ copies of THE CATHOLIC YOUTH BIBLE or another Bible, one for each participant (optional)
- Mark the Scripture reading (Luke 6:36–42) in a Bible.
- Select one or more readers to proclaim the three readings.

Procedure

Step 1: Overview of Process and Creation of Faith-Sharing Groups

Introduce the faith sharing with Scripture process using these or similar words:

- ○ This faith-sharing experience is adapted from an ancient Catholic prayer style called *lectio divina,* or "divine reading." This prayerful reading invites us to open ourselves up to Scripture so that God may speak to us as well as through us to others around us.

○ The process follows a simple formula. We will listen to the proclamation of a short Scripture passage three times. I will suggest a focus for your reflection during each reading. After each you will be invited to share some thoughts that came to mind during the reading. When it is your turn, please say "pass" if you do not wish to share.

If the group size is larger than ten, divide into small faith-sharing groups of five to seven. Select one person in each faith-sharing group to serve as a prayer leader.

Distribute paper and pens or pencils to each participant. If you are providing participants with bibles, distribute those also.

Step 2: Introduction and Reading One

Introduce this faith-sharing experience by inviting the participants to quiet themselves and focus on their breathing. Ask them to spend a full 30 seconds simply listening to their breathing, and then offer the following introductory prayer:

○ Word of God, gift us with ears to hear your words and hearts that will seek your wisdom.

Proceed with the comments below:

○ Listen closely to this reading from the Gospel of Luke as Jesus speaks to the crowd about forgiveness and judgment. As you listen, reflect on the judgments you might have made this past week and open yourself to the one word that God is trying to speak to you today about forgiveness. Please select only one word. When the reading is finished, each of you will be invited to share your word with your small group.

Invite the designated reader to proclaim Luke 6:36–42 slowly and prayerfully to the group.

Step 3: Sharing One Word

Invite the participants to share the one word they selected during the reading with the members of their small group. Ask the prayer leader in each group to begin. Remind everyone to share just the one word.

Step 4: Reading Two

Prepare everyone for the second reading using these or similar words:

○ During the second proclamation of the passage, listen for the phrase or sentence that God is trying to speak to you today. It does not have to contain the word that you just shared. When the reading is finished,

each of you will have an opportunity to share that phrase with your small group.

Invite the designated reader to proclaim Luke 6:36–42 slowly and prayerfully to the group.

Step 5: Sharing the Phrase

Invite each small-group prayer leader to share her or his phrase, and then give everyone else in the small group an opportunity to share their phrases. Remind everyone to share just the phrase, without further explanation.

Step 6: Reading Three

Prepare everyone for the third reading using these or similar words:
  o Listen to the reading one last time. Open yourself up to how God is asking you to apply this reading to your life today. When the reading is finished, you will have some time to reflect on what God is saying to you and to share your reflection with your group if you wish.

Invite the designated reader to proclaim Luke 6:36–42 slowly and prayerfully to the group.

Step 7: Sharing the Reflection

Explain to the participants that they will now have a short period of silence to reflect on what God is saying to them. Invite them to use the paper to write thoughts or draw images that come to mind during the reflection period. After a minute or two of quiet reflection, invite the participants to begin sharing their reflections in their small groups using the mutual invitation process.

Note: If the participants are unfamiliar with this process, take a minute to summarize the description on page 10 (see "Using the Mutual Invitation Process to Share Faith" in the introduction). Be sure to remind them of the option to pass.

Allow several minutes for this sharing.

Step 8: Conclusion and Closing Prayer

Conclude with these or similar words:
  o The Lord's Prayer is perhaps one of the best prayers of forgiveness that we can offer to God and to one another.

  o We face a challenge when we say "Amen!" to this statement: As we pray, we ask God to forgive us just as much as we are forgiving others!

○ Let us take up that challenge together, by joining hands and daring to pray these words to our God, who is ready and waiting to forgive us as much as we will allow it.

Lead the participants in praying the Lord's Prayer together.

Scripture 10
Discipleship

Scripture: John 13:1–5,12–17

Overview

This faith-sharing experience invites young people to reflect on discipleship and what it means to follow Jesus today. The process focuses on one of the most powerful and poignant readings from the Gospel of John—the washing of the disciples' feet—where Jesus demonstrates that service lies at the heart of discipleship.

Estimated Time: 15–20 minutes

Preparation Steps

- Gather the following items:
  - ☐ paper and a pen or pencil for each participant
  - ☐ copies of THE CATHOLIC YOUTH BIBLE or another Bible, one for each participant (optional)
- Mark the Scripture reading (John 13:1–5,12–17) in a Bible.
- Select one or more readers to proclaim the three readings.

Procedure

Step 1: Overview of Process and Creation of Faith-Sharing Groups

Introduce the faith sharing with Scripture process using these or similar words:

- ○ This faith-sharing experience is adapted from an ancient Catholic prayer style called *lectio divina,* or "divine reading." This prayerful

reading invites us to open ourselves up to Scripture so that God may speak to us as well as through us to others around us.

- The process follows a simple formula. We will listen to the proclamation of a short Scripture passage three times. I will suggest a focus for your reflection during each reading. After each you will be invited to share some thoughts that came to mind during the reading. When it is your turn, please say "pass" if you do not wish to share.

If the group size is larger than ten, divide into small faith-sharing groups of five to seven. Select one person in each faith-sharing group to serve as a prayer leader.

Distribute paper and pens or pencils to each participant. If you are providing participants with bibles, distribute those also.

Step 2: Introduction and Reading One

Introduce this faith-sharing experience by inviting the participants to quiet themselves and focus on their breathing. Ask them to spend a full 30 seconds simply listening to their breathing, and then offer the following introductory prayer:

- Word of God, gift us with ears to hear your words and hearts that will seek your wisdom.

Proceed with the comments below:

- Listen closely to this reading from the Gospel of John, which tells of Jesus washing the feet of his disciples and his command that we should wash one another's feet. Jesus's model of service presents a challenging image of what it means to be a disciple. As you listen, reflect on how God is calling you to serve others in this coming week and open yourself to the one word that God is trying to speak to you today about discipleship. Please select only one word. When the reading is finished, each of you will be invited to share your word with your small group.

Invite the designated reader to proclaim John 13:1–5,12–17 slowly and prayerfully to the group.

Step 3: Sharing One Word

Invite the participants to share the one word they selected during the reading with the members of their small group. Ask the prayer leader in each group to begin. Remind everyone to share just the one word.

Step 4: Reading Two

Prepare everyone for the second reading using these or similar words:
- ○ During the second proclamation of the passage, listen for the phrase or sentence that God is trying to speak to you today. It does not have to contain the word that you just shared. When the reading is finished, each of you will have an opportunity to share that phrase with your small group.

Invite the designated reader to proclaim John 13:1–5,12–17 slowly and prayerfully to the group.

Step 5: Sharing the Phrase

Invite each small-group prayer leader to share his or her phrase, and then give everyone else in the small group an opportunity to share their phrases. Remind everyone to share just the phrase, without further explanation.

Step 6: Reading Three

Prepare everyone for the third reading using these or similar words:
- ○ Listen to the reading one last time. Open yourself up to how God is asking you to apply this reading to your life today. When the reading is finished, you will have some time to reflect on what God is saying to you and to share your reflection with your group if you wish.

Invite the designated reader to proclaim John 13:1–5,12–17 slowly and prayerfully to the group.

Step 7: Sharing the Reflection

Explain to the participants that they will now have a short period of silence to reflect on what God is saying to them. Invite them to use the paper to write thoughts or draw images that come to mind during the reflection period. After a minute or two of quiet reflection, invite the participants to begin sharing their reflections in their small groups using the mutual invitation process.

Note: If the participants are unfamiliar with this process, take a minute to summarize the description on page 10 (see "Using the Mutual Invitation Process to Share Faith" in the introduction). Be sure to remind them of the option to pass.

Allow several minutes for this sharing.

Step 8: Conclusion and Closing Prayer

Conclude with these or similar words:

- The image of Jesus washing the disciples' feet is powerful and challenging.

- To say that we believe in and follow a God who would humble himself to do this says a lot about what we are called to do in his name.

- As we pray together, let us conclude by reflecting on how God is calling us to serve others during the coming week.

Invite everyone to pray the Lord's Prayer together.

Part Two

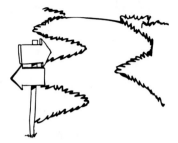

Faith Sharing with Guided Meditation

What Is Guided Meditation?

Guided meditation is an intentional process of reflection that uses relaxation and guided imagery. The leader of the process invites participants to allow themselves to be led on a journey of faith, during which they are asked to reflect on an imaginative story or Scripture passage, an issue of concern, or an aspect of their life. The keys to a successful guided meditation experience include creating a relaxed environment for participants and reading the meditation script in a calm tone and at a slow pace.

Preparing the Environment

Although guided meditations can be done just about anywhere, they are most effectively done in a place that is free from external distractions, such as outside noises, people entering or leaving the room, or people whispering or giggling. Before you begin to read the meditation, dim or turn off the lights and invite the participants to find a comfortable place and posture that will not disrupt others. Playing reflective music in the background (soft instrumental music without words) may also help to minimize distractions and create a calm environment. Wait until a quiet, reflective mood has been established before beginning the reading of the meditation.

Reading the Meditation Script

It is very important to read the script slowly and to pause when you see a set of ellipsis marks (. . .). The best way to make sure you are taking the right amount of time is to close your eyes when you encounter an ellipsis mark and imagine yourself on the journey in the script. If you can see and feel what you are asking the rest of the group to see and feel, then you are pausing for an appropriate amount of time. Occasionally, there is a directive in the script to pause for a longer amount of time (e.g., *"Pause for 30 seconds here*"). It is important to honor the designated time frame when you see these directives.

One of the biggest mistakes made in attempting guided meditation is reading too fast. This includes the introductory paragraphs that invite the participants to relax and focus on their breathing. Once everyone is quiet and still, read the script in a deliberately calm voice, allowing the participants to interpret the image or scene as their own imagination leads them.

The Best Settings for Guided Meditations

Of the faith-sharing processes outlined in this book, guided meditations require the most time. Twenty minutes is suggested, but more time may be needed, depending on the maturity and trust level of the group. Guided meditations will not be effective if they are rushed or squeezed into the last minutes of a class or other session. The optimal time for guided meditations for faith sharing is at the very beginning or near the end of a class or session, when the leader does not feel rushed about getting to the next objective or task. During retreats, evenings are a particularly good time for guided meditations because group dynamics and trust have been well enough established so that participants can "let go" and fully enter the guided process.

Guided Meditation 1
And the Word Became Flesh

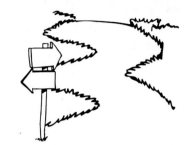

Scripture: John 1:1–5,14

Overview

There is tremendous power in a word. In this meditation based on selected passages from John's Gospel, the participants meet and talk with Jesus, who ends up writing a word on the palms of their hands. The power of the word Jesus writes is unique for each person. In the sharing that follows the meditation, the participants will explore the meaning of the word they receive.

Estimated Time: 20 minutes

Preparation Steps

- Gather the following items:
    - ☐ one washable marker for each participant (avoid yellow and other light colors)
    - ☐ THE CATHOLIC YOUTH BIBLE or another Bible
- Mark the Scripture reading (John 1:1–5,14) in a Bible and select a reader to proclaim it during step 5.
- Play a CD of reflective instrumental music (optional).

Procedure

Step 1: Creation of Faith-Sharing Groups

Divide into small groups of five to seven, and select one person in each group to serve as the prayer leader. Distribute a washable marker to each person.

Step 2: Focus the Group

Dim the lights, if possible. Play a CD of instrumental music, if you have that option. Begin the meditation with these or similar words:

- Find a comfortable place to sit where you can be quiet and relaxed and will not be disturbed. It is important to position yourself where you will not be distracted by anyone while the guided meditation is taking place.

Wait until everyone has found their place and position and all movement and talking have stopped before proceeding with the meditation.

Step 3: Read the Meditation Script

Slowly read the following script:

- Close your eyes and take a deep and slow breath in . . . and exhale slowly . . . Breathe in deeply once more . . . and exhale slowly. . . . Feel your body relaxing . . . as your mind is cleared of all the thoughts that have filled it up until this moment. . . . Continue to listen to your breath as you slowly take in air . . . and slowly and quietly release it . . .

- Picture yourself walking up a hillside. . . . You are alone, and there is no rush to do anything in particular. . . . Just relax in the present moment of this perfect day. . . . The air is warm and the sun feels good upon your arms . . . your neck . . . and your back. . . . You can hear the birds in the trees as you pass by . . . and smell the aroma of the wildflowers that surround your path. . . . Your eyes are set upon a bench that is underneath a shade tree at the top of the hill. . . . It almost seems to call out to you to come and rest a while . . .

- As you near the top of the hill, you sit down on the bench and look out at the wondrous landscape that lies before you . . . the gently rolling hills . . . the birds gliding effortlessly in the air . . . the soft breeze blowing through your hair. . . . You lean back to take in the perfection of this moment, and you see a person walking up the hill toward you. . . . He too is taking his time, looking intently and carefully at everything he passes. . . . He lifts his eyes to meet yours, and you know in your heart that this is Jesus. . . . As his eyes catch yours, a reassuring smile comes across his face. . . . He knows you . . . and he has come to talk with you for a while . . .

- As he nears the place where you are sitting, he motions for you to stay seated and asks if he can join you on the bench. . . . He sits down next to you and for a few moments says nothing; he just takes in the beauty of the scenery that surrounds him. . . . Turning toward you, Jesus asks how you are doing. . . . He wants to know how you are *really* doing. . . . He wants to know about the things that seem to be troubling you at this point in your life. . . . You know you can trust him with anything, so you begin to tell him the things that are on your mind, the problems that are waiting for you when you go back down the hill and return to your home, your friends, and your school . . .

(Pause for one full minute here.)

o As you share your thoughts and concerns with Jesus, you sense that he is listening to you as no other person has before. . . . His eyes never leave you, never wander away from you as you speak . . . never condemn you. . . . It's as if you are the only person in the world right now. . . . As you finish sharing your concerns with Jesus, you are sure that he understands you . . . that he knows the depth and the importance of all that you've shared with him. . . . And you wait for him to reply . . .

o He holds up a finger and tells you that the answers you seek can be found in one word that he wants to trace on the palm of your hand. . . . He gently reaches for your hand and writes the word with his finger on your palm. . . . As he forms each letter, your eyes and your heart begin to understand what the word is . . . and recognize its meaning. . . . He clasps both of your hands in his and holds them as he stares into your eyes. . . . He asks you to never let go of this word . . . to let it be a reminder to you that you do not walk this journey alone, that he is with you, especially during the hard parts. . . . With that, he lays his hand on your head and blesses you and asks you to return down the hillside so that you can bring to life the word that he gave to you. . . . Then he turns and walks back down the hillside. . . . As Jesus walks on, you use your marker to slowly trace over the letters that Jesus has written on your hand . . . feeling his finger trace each letter as you take in the full meaning of the word he is asking you to live . . .

o Now become aware of your breathing . . . and your presence in this room . . . in this moment. . . . Slowly open your eyes and breathe deeply in . . . and out . . . and look at your palm and focus on the word that Jesus has written in the palm of your hand . . .

Step 4: Small-Group Faith Sharing

Ask everyone to return to their small group. Once everyone is settled, continue with these or similar words:

o Each prayer leader will begin the faith sharing by showing the word written in her or his palm and sharing the meaning it has for her or him this week. Each group member should share in the same manner, using the mutual invitation process.

Note: If the participants are unfamiliar with the mutual invitation process, take a minute to summarize the description on page 10 (see "Using the

Mutual Invitation Process to Share Faith" in the introduction). Be sure to remind them of the option to pass if they prefer not to share.

Allow several minutes for this sharing.

Step 5: Conclusion and Closing Prayer

Conclude with these or similar words:

- ○ We will now hear the proclamation of several passages from the Gospel of John. As you listen, focus on the word written on your hand and think about what you need from God in order to bring that word to life during the coming week.

Invite the designated reader to proclaim John 1:1–5,14.

Invite the participants to say aloud a worry, concern, or request they would like to place in God's hands this week. Invite them to complete this sentence starter: "Lord, into your hands I place . . . "

Close by inviting everyone to join hands and pray the Lord's Prayer.

Guided Meditation 2
Come to Dinner

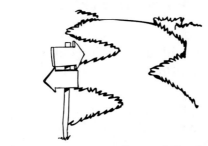

Scripture: Luke 19:1–10

Overview

In this meditation and small-group sharing exercise, the participants can reflect on a modern-day Zacchaeus scenario unfolding at their school. They are invited to consider what transformation might occur in their own lives if Jesus were to ask them to share a meal with him.

Estimated Time: 20 minutes

Preparation Steps

- Mark the Scripture reading (Luke 19:1–10) in a Bible and select a reader to proclaim it during step 4.
- Play a CD of reflective instrumental music (optional).

Procedure

Step 1: Creation of Faith-Sharing Groups

Divide into small groups of five to seven, and select one person in each group to serve as the prayer leader.

Step 2: Focus the Group

Dim the lights, if possible. Play a CD of instrumental music, if you have that option. Begin the meditation with these or similar words:
  - Find a comfortable place to sit where you can be quiet and relaxed and will not be disturbed. It is important to position yourself where you will not be distracted by anyone while the guided meditation is taking place.

Wait until everyone has found their place and position and all movement and talking have stopped before proceeding with the meditation.

Step 3: Read the Meditation Script

Slowly read the meditation script:

○ Close your eyes and take a deep and slow breath in . . . and exhale slowly. . . . Breathe in deeply once more . . . and exhale slowly. . . . Feel your body relaxing . . . as your mind is cleared of all the thoughts that have filled it up until this moment. . . . Continue to listen to your breath as you slowly take in air . . . and slowly and quietly release it . . .

○ It is around noon, and you are having lunch in the cafeteria at school, sitting with the same group you always do . . . talking about what has happened as well as what might happen in the coming week with school . . . your friends . . . upcoming events . . . and even people with whom you don't get along so well . . .

○ Suddenly a buzz begins near the door . . . some sort of commotion is occurring in the hallway. . . . At first you think a fight has broken out, but then you hear someone say, "He's here!" Other voices shout out, "Why did he come?" . . . "What does he want?" . . . "I can't believe he is in this building!" . . . You join the crowd that is quickly gathering in the hallway. . . . You hear people in the front begin to shout excitedly, "It's Jesus!" "He's come to our school!" . . . At first you think it's a joke, perhaps a senior prank, but your curiosity is stronger than your doubt and you push forward. . . . But the crowd is too thick now . . . everyone wants to see Jesus . . . some are calling out to him . . . wanting to catch his attention . . . wanting to speak with him. . . . You find yourself pulled between calling out and wanting to hide from him . . . worried what he might say or do if you actually end up face to face with him in front of your friends or, even worse, in front of those who would take joy in your embarrassment . . .

○ You decide to take the risk . . . you don't want this once-in-a-lifetime opportunity to pass you by. . . . You climb up on a table that other people are standing on in order to get a better look, but it's still hard for you to see. . . . You find a chair and place it on top of the table and awkwardly climb onto it. . . . Finally, you have a good vantage point from which to see over everyone in the crowd . . . and then Jesus walks by. . . . He is walking slowly, looking from side to side as he goes down the hall, as if he's looking for someone . . . but you wonder who he could possibly be interested in finding at this school . . .

○ Just then he stops and turns toward you. . . . The crowd follows his gaze and sees that he is looking at you . . . and only you . . . and the room becomes momentarily silent. . . . It reminds you of the calm before the storm, and your first impulse is to run and hide, but there is nowhere to run. . . . Then someone shouts out for all to hear, "Why is he looking at that person?" . . . Another person, one who is not your friend, shouts, "Doesn't he know the things that person has done?!" . . . The comment causes you to think about your life . . . especially the times when you turned your back on your beliefs in favor of some immediate attention and escape . . . and how you hurt others with your words and actions . . . and you wonder to yourself, "Why is he looking at me? What does he want?" . . . You expect him to smirk and look away or pronounce judgment against you . . . but to your surprise, his eyes never leave yours and he seems unfazed by the comments from the crowd. . . . In fact, he steps toward you as the crowd parts. . . . He stands before the table you are on and loudly speaks your name so all can hear it. . . . Hearing your name come from his lips catches you off guard . . . and many others in the crowd off guard, too. . . . "He knows *my* name?" you wonder to yourself, surprised by the caring way in which he speaks to you. . . . Then he says he wants to have dinner with you . . . at *your* home . . . tonight! . . .

- People begin to murmur and gossip among themselves, but their comments quickly fade into nothingness as Jesus continues to look up at you . . . never averting his eyes from yours, awaiting your response. . . . Awestruck, you nod "yes" as you wonder about the miracle of this moment—Jesus wanting to share a meal with you . . . at your house!

- Jesus helps you down from the table and leads you through the crowd. . . . Stares of unbelief and shock are frozen on the faces you pass. . . . As you leave school and walk toward your home, you begin to have a long conversation with Jesus about the past year, especially the struggles you've had lately in your life . . .

(Pause for 15 seconds here.)

- By the time you enter your home, you feel alive and renewed. . . . Jesus listened to all you had to say and didn't condemn you . . . didn't change his mind about wanting to be seen with you. . . . As you sit down to have dinner, Jesus begins to speak to you about your life . . . about the worries that you have shared with him . . . and about the shortcomings you have confided to him. . . . And the truth of his words fills you with life . . . and hope . . .

(Pause for 15 seconds here.)

- As he speaks, you feel a change taking place within you . . . from the inside. . . . It is an overwhelming need to make things right . . . to change your life and turn things around in the days and weeks ahead. . . . It turns your attention on the people you need to forgive . . . as well as the people and things that need to be given more attention. . . . You think about what needs to happen in the coming week for you to begin reordering your life . . . to let others know that you have been transformed by the Good News of Jesus . . .

- Now become aware of your breathing . . . and your presence in this room . . . in this moment. . . . Slowly open your eyes and breathe deeply in . . . and out . . . and reflect on what transformation needs to occur in your life in the coming week.

Step 4: Proclamation of Scripture

Introduce the reading from Luke with these or similar words:
- Keep the meditation you just completed fresh in your mind as you listen to a story from Scripture that tells how the presence of Jesus transformed a hurting and lonely heart.

Invite the designated reader to proclaim Luke 19:1–10.
Introduce a few moments of silent reflection with these words:
- Think about the power of second chances and new directions that may have struck you during the meditation and the Scripture story. Take a minute to silently reflect on the meaning of this for you and for your life this week.

Step 5: Small-Group Faith Sharing

Ask everyone to return to their small group. Once everyone is settled, continue with these or similar words:
- Both the guided meditation and the Scripture story of Zacchaeus provide us with lots of food for thought on the theme of new directions. As you prepare to share with those in small groups, try to focus on one key insight or prevailing image about the power of getting a second chance to walk in a new direction. In which direction do you wish to walk during the coming week?

Invite the participants to share their insights or images about second chances and new directions using the mutual invitation process.

Note: If the participants are unfamiliar with the mutual invitation process, take a minute to summarize the description on page 10 (see "Using the Mutual Invitation Process to Share Faith" in the introduction). Be sure to remind them of the option to pass.

Step 6: Conclusion and Closing Prayer

Conclude with these or similar words:
- In the story of Zacchaeus, Jesus shows not only the power of sharing a meal but the power of invitation, as well. Perhaps your meditation also provided you with a vision of the transforming influence that Jesus can have in our lives.
- Consider what you need this week to make a fresh start, to take a new path or direction that leads you closer to Jesus.
- As we conclude this time together, I invite each of you to offer a prayer petition completing the phrase, "Lord, walk with me toward _____."

Close by inviting everyone to pray the Lord's Prayer together.

Guided Meditation 3
Lost and Found

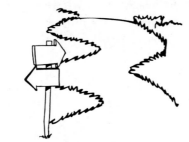

Scripture: Luke 15:1–7

Overview

This meditation takes young people on a journey in which they become lost in a maze of sin and selfishness. As Jesus breaks through the walls of the maze, he leads the participants toward the forgiveness and love that await each of them. This meditation can also serve as an examination of conscience when one is celebrating the sacrament of Penance and Reconciliation.

Estimated Time: 20 minutes

Preparation Steps

- Gather the following items:
    - ☐ paper and a pen or pencil for each participant
    - ☐ THE CATHOLIC YOUTH BIBLE or another Bible
- Mark the Scripture reading (Luke 15:1–7) in a Bible and select a reader to proclaim it during step 5.
- Play a CD of reflective instrumental music (optional).

Procedure

Step 1: Creation of Faith-Sharing Groups

Divide into small groups of five to seven, and select one person in each group to serve as the prayer leader.

Step 2: Focus the Group

Dim the lights, if possible. Play a CD of instrumental music, if you have that option. Begin the meditation with these or similar words:
- ○ Find a comfortable place to sit where you can be quiet and relaxed and will not be disturbed. It is important to position yourself where you will not be distracted by anyone while the guided meditation is taking place.

Wait until everyone has found their place and position and all movement and talking have stopped before proceeding with the meditation.

Step 3: Read the Meditation Script

Slowly read the following script:
- ○ Close your eyes and take a deep and slow breath in . . . and exhale slowly. . . . Breathe in deeply once more . . . and exhale slowly. . . . Feel your body relaxing . . . as your mind is cleared of all the thoughts that have filled it up until this moment. . . . Continue to listen to your breath as you slowly take in air . . . and slowly and quietly release it . . .
- ○ You find yourself lost in the middle of a maze of high walls. . . . You are alone, and you cannot see over or climb over the walls to find your way back to the beginning. . . . Every time you turn a corner, you are confronted with another wall, each one bearing a word that somehow connects to your life. . . . On the first wall, the word *ignore* is written, and you think about a time when you had an opportunity to help someone who was hurting but chose to ignore the person. . . . You remember the situation . . . being in a hurry, feeling conflict about what you should do . . . ultimately deciding to look the other way and not get involved. . . . Now you wish that you had stopped and spent the few minutes it would have taken to help heal the hurt . . .
- ○ As you turn left, you see a wall with the word *hurt* written on it, and you think about a time when you let down a friend who was depending on your friendship and trust; only this time, you feel the hurt that your friend felt when you were not around . . .
- ○ The reality of the other person's pain makes you want to get out of the maze. . . . You run ahead, darting left and then right, suddenly coming face to face with a wall on which the word *used* is written . . . and you remember a time when you took advantage of another person for your own gain and status. . . . Feelings of sorrow and regret begin to overcome you. . . . You become desperate to find a way out of this maze, to find the safety of home . . .
- ○ You stumble around another corner and see a wall with the word *greed* on it. . . . You are confused at first because you are not a greedy person . . . but then you think about how much you

spend on things . . . at the mall . . . online . . . at the convenience store. . . . Some of these things are unnecessary, some maybe even harmful, but all of them fill your life, your room, your body with more than you need or should use. . . . You feel anger rising within you; you've been made to feel guilty by this maze of walls. . . . You yell at God about how unfair life is . . . how demanding God is . . . and how mean and uncaring the world is. . . . You stomp off toward the opposite end of the maze and come upon a cracked and broken wall with the word *anger* on it, and then you see the word *hatred* spray painted below that. . . . Slowly, names of people you have resented over the years appear on the wall. The list grows to include whole groups of people that you cannot stand or have tried to avoid in your life: those of other colors, cultures, and perceived reputations and those who just seem odd or strange to you. . . . You find yourself wanting to give up . . . not knowing how or even caring whether you can escape this maze of sin and selfishness . . . feeling trapped, with no chance of escape . . .

○ Just as you are ready to give up, the wall of hatred and anger before you tumbles to the ground . . . and Jesus is standing there . . . holding out his arms . . . calling your name . . . inviting you to come toward him and his embrace. . . . You slowly rise and begin to step toward his call. . . . With each step you quicken your pace, until you are running toward him . . . eyes wet with sorrow and pain. . . . You lunge into his arms . . . as you let out a loud cry of grief and sorrow, which is muffled and then silenced as Jesus engulfs you with his embrace. . . . You've never been held so tightly before. . . . You relax and lie in his arms as he picks you up and carries you toward the end of the maze. . . . As he walks, walls simply vanish or crumble before him, and within seconds, the maze is gone . . . replaced by a grassy field where sheep graze and birds fly overhead. . . . He turns to you and simply says your name . . . and adds, "You were lost, but now you have been found . . . rejoice and welcome home" . . .

○ You breathe in deeply the presence and peacefulness of this place . . . of this moment . . . and inside you know that this next week will be different . . . that you will avoid getting trapped in the maze again . . .

○ Now become aware of your breathing . . . and your presence in this room . . . in this moment. . . . Slowly open your eyes and breathe deeply in . . . and out . . . slowly and consciously . . . aware of this moment and God's presence with us now . . .

Step 4: Individual Reflection and Small-Group Faith Sharing

Ask everyone to return to their small group. Distribute paper and pens or pencils. Once everyone is settled, continue with these or similar words:

○ Spend a few moments reflecting on some of the walls that have separated you from others this past week.

○ Use your paper to draw an image of the maze that you find yourself caught up in lately.

Continue by inviting the participants to share in their small groups using the mutual invitation process. Ask them to show the others all or part of the maze they have drawn and to briefly explain the meaning and significance of the part they share.

Note: If the participants are unfamiliar with the mutual invitation process, take a minute to summarize the description on page 10 (see "Using the Mutual Invitation Process to Share Faith" in the introduction). Be sure to remind them of the option to pass.

Allow several minutes for this sharing.

Step 5: Conclusion and Closing Prayer

Continue with these or similar words:

○ We will now hear the proclamation of a reading from the Gospel of Luke.

○ As you listen, look at the maze you have drawn and think about where you are and where God is in that drawing.

Invite the designated reader to proclaim Luke 15:1–7.

After the reading has been proclaimed, invite the young people to conclude the session by offering a prayer petition to which the group responds, "Good Shepherd, carry us home."

Guided Meditation 4
The Treasure Left Behind

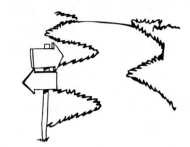

Scripture: Luke 12:29–34

Overview

What difference will your life make in this world? This is an important question for young people to consider as they discern a mission in life and determine the values and beliefs that will guide them. This meditation experience invites young people to begin at the end of their lives, reflecting on what they imagine those close to them might say about the difference their life made in this world, as well as the values and beliefs that formed the foundation for that difference.

Estimated Time: 20 minutes

Preparation Steps

- Gather the following items:
  - ☐ paper and a pen or pencil for each participant
  - ☐ THE CATHOLIC YOUTH BIBLE or another Bible
- Mark the Scripture reading (Luke 12:29–34) in a Bible and select a reader to proclaim it during step 5.
- Play a CD of reflective instrumental music (optional).

Procedure

Step 1: Creation of Faith-Sharing Groups

Divide the group into small groups of five to seven, and select one person in each group to serve as the prayer leader.

Step 2: Focus the Group

Dim the lights, if possible. Play a CD of instrumental music, if you have that option. Begin the meditation with these or similar words:

- ○ Find a comfortable place to sit where you can be quiet and relaxed and will not be disturbed. It is important to position yourself where you will not be distracted by anyone while the guided meditation is taking place.

Wait until everyone has found their place and position and all movement and talking have stopped before proceeding with the meditation.

Step 3: Read the Meditation Script

Slowly read the following script:

- ○ Close your eyes and take a deep and slow breath in . . . and exhale slowly. . . . Breathe in deeply once more . . . and exhale slowly. . . . Feel your body relaxing . . . as your mind is cleared of all the thoughts that have filled it up until this moment. . . . Continue to listen to your breath as you slowly take in air . . . and slowly and quietly release it . . .

- ○ Imagine that it is your seventy-fifth birthday . . . you are entering the sunset of your life. . . . Notice how the years have changed your appearance . . . but have not altered your mind or spirit. . . . You look around and find yourself surrounded by all the people, family and friends, who have been a part of those seventy-five years. . . . You recognize many of the faces from as far back as when you were in high school, some sixty years ago . . .

- ○ One by one . . . people bring you a gift, not a material one but a gift of remembrance. . . . Each gift is a testimony to who you have become over your seventy-five years . . . a testimony to the difference you made in their lives . . . and to the values and beliefs you lived out during that time . . .

- ○ The first person to come forward is your oldest child, now grown and with children of her own. . . . She shares with you and the rest of the group one of the key values that you helped instill in her as she grew through her teen years. . . . What is the value that she speaks about to the group?

- ○ Next, one of your grandchildren comes forward, one who is now a teenager himself. . . . In fact, he has your eyes and very much reminds you of yourself when you were his age. . . . He shares the gift of your wisdom . . . and tells the group what you have taught him to believe about life and faith. . . . What is it that he says to the group?

- ○ The next person to step forward is someone that you worked with for a number of years. . . . This person offers a few jokes about the "early years" together and then proceeds to tell the group of the gift

you have been to others by the job you chose and what you did with
it. . . . What does this coworker share with the group about your
choice of careers and what you chose to do with your education?

o The pastor from your parish steps forward to speak about your faith
and your service to the parish and the community. . . . He speaks
of your prayer life and your commitment to the community of
faith. . . . What does he say about all of this to the crowd that is
gathered?

o Finally, your spouse of nearly fifty years steps forward and holds your
hand. . . . You look at this person as you did on your wedding day,
remembering the blank canvas of possibilities on which you began
to paint together. . . . You smile as your spouse begins to tell
about some of the more memorable moments of life together with
you. . . . What does your spouse say about your strengths? . . . your
weaknesses? . . . your dreams? . . . and your regrets? . . .

o Now it is your turn to speak to the crowd of family and
friends. . . . You speak of the way your tried to live your
beliefs . . . your faith . . . and your values . . . and you sum it up
in a phrase that you ask to have written on your tombstone when you
are gone . . . a phrase that will tell generations who read it what was
most important in your life, as well as which values and beliefs had
the most meaning for your life . . .

o Now become aware of your breathing . . . and your presence in this
room . . . in this moment. . . . Slowly open your eyes and breathe
deeply in . . . and out . . .

Step 4: Individual Reflection and Small-Group Faith Sharing

Ask everyone to return to their small group. Distribute paper and pens or
pencils. Once everyone is settled, continue with these or similar words:

o Spend a moment recalling some of the phrases that came to mind
during the meditation.

o Write down the one that does the best job of summarizing what is
most important to you and names the values and beliefs that will mark
your life in this world. In a couple of minutes, you will be invited to
share this phrase with the small group.

Continue by inviting the participants to share their phrases in their small
groups using the mutual invitation process.

Note: If the participants are unfamiliar with the mutual invitation process,
take a minute to summarize the description on page 10 (see "Using the
Mutual Invitation Process to Share Faith" in the introduction). Be sure to
remind them of the option to pass.

Allow several minutes for this sharing.

Step 5: Conclusion and Closing Prayer

Conclude with these or similar words:

○ We will now hear a reading from the Gospel of Luke. As you listen, reflect on what difference you want your life to make in this world and what kind of treasure you want to be remembered for in your life.

Invite the designated reader to proclaim Luke 12:29–34.

Close by inviting the young people to name one thing they would like to be remembered for in life, using the phrase, "Lord, let my gift to the world be _____."

After each person has shared, conclude with the following prayer:

○ God of all good gifts, we lift these hopes and dreams up to you and ask you to give us the fortitude and patience to live a life worthy of being called your followers. We ask this through Christ, our risen Lord. Amen.

Guided Meditation 5
Hand Delivered

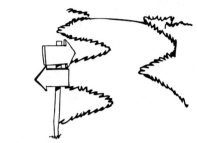

Scripture: Psalm 40:2–9

Overview

In this meditation, participants are invited to confront the demons of doubt by letting go and trusting in the presence of God, even when God cannot be seen.

Estimated Time: 15–20 minutes

Preparation Steps

- Gather the following items:
  - ☐ paper and a pen or pencil for each participant
  - ☐ THE CATHOLIC YOUTH BIBLE or another Bible
- Mark the Scripture reading (Psalm 40:2–9) in a Bible and select a reader to proclaim it during step 5.
- Play a CD of reflective instrumental music (optional).

Procedure

Step 1: Creation of Faith-Sharing Groups

Divide the group into small groups of five to seven, and select one person in each group to serve as the prayer leader.

Step 2: Focus the Group

Dim the lights, if possible. Play a CD of instrumental music, if you have that option. Begin the meditation with these or similar words:

- Find a comfortable place to sit where you can be quiet and relaxed and will not be disturbed. It is important to position yourself where you will not be distracted by anyone while the guided meditation is taking place.

Wait until everyone has found their place and position and all movement and talking have stopped before proceeding with the meditation.

Step 3: Read the Meditation Script

Slowly read the following script:

- Close your eyes and take a deep and slow breath in . . . and exhale slowly. . . . Breathe in deeply once more . . . and exhale slowly. . . . Feel your body relaxing . . . as your mind is cleared of all the thoughts that have filled it up until this moment. . . . Continue to listen to your breath as you slowly take in air . . . and slowly and quietly release it . . .

- Imagine yourself walking along the edge of the Grand Canyon. . . . As you look out into the canyon, you can see the beautiful red and brown glow of the rocks for miles around. . . . The birds soar at eye level and the clouds drift nearby, some so close that you can almost reach out and touch them. . . . The sun is warm on your neck and face and the wind is still. . . . You stroll along effortlessly, taking in a view so magnificent that you cannot describe it in words . . . realizing that it must be seen and felt with the heart . . . and with the soul . . .

- As you turn to walk down a path, you notice a quick movement in the brush behind you. . . . A slight feeling of uneasiness begins to rise within you as you peer closely into the thick brush. . . . Suddenly, a figure moves toward you and you immediately turn and run, not knowing the identity of the figure but feeling a definite sense of fear. . . . The creature calls out to you, knows your name, and commands you to stop. . . . But somehow you know that if you stop running, this creature will overtake you . . . and your soul. . . . You continue running full speed down the path as the creature screams behind you that there is no escape . . . that it knows your weaknesses . . . your fears . . . and even begins to call out some of them . . .

- As you leap over a small ravine, you wonder how this creature knows your deepest fears and failings . . . how it seems to know the darkness of your soul and the doubts in your mind. . . . The creature's familiarity with you and your life begins to frighten you even more than the creature itself. . . . You glance back and notice that the creature seems to be growing in size and getting closer to you with each stride . . . and you begin to understand that the creature grows at the same rate as your own fears and doubts . . .

○ As you make a quick right, you suddenly find yourself at the edge of the canyon ledge with nowhere else to run. . . . You turn, trapped and out of breath, finally facing the creature who has now doubled in size and stands towering over you only steps away. . . . The creature grins and lets out a sharp laugh that echoes off the canyon walls, sending a haunting sensation down your spine. . . . The creature tells you that the chase is over . . . that there is no escape from the ugly truth . . . and commands you to give in to the darkness that is already a part of you. . . . You are about to give up . . . to give in to the creature's wishes, when somewhere behind you there is a whisper . . .

○ You turn around to see only a dark void over the canyon ledge . . . yet you hear the remnants of the soft whisper still rising from the depths below. . . . It seems to say, "Let go." . . . You bend over to try and peer deeper into the darkness, to be sure you are not hearing things. . . . You wait . . . and listen . . . as a clearer voice from the darkness drifts up toward you. . . . "Let go, trust me," it says. . . . You turn toward the creature, who now seems somewhat hesitant about moving forward. . . . You shout into the darkness, "Who are you? Where are you?" But the reply is the same, "Let go . . . trust me."

○ Suddenly, the creature becomes agitated and angry, and letting out a loud growl, leaps forward, grabbing at you. . . . In that moment, you decide that there is only one choice . . . a choice to trust . . . and opening wide your arms . . . you fall backward . . . into the darkness below, as the creature follows you over the cliff. . . . The fall immediately takes your breath away . . . as if you have just plunged down the first big hill on a giant roller coaster. . . . You are trying to catch your breath, hoping, praying for an end to the helplessness of the freefall you are in . . .

○ Then you feel your body come into contact with something soft . . . as if you have fallen onto a cloud . . . but it is still dark and you cannot see anything. . . . You have the sense of being carried by someone . . . someone who cares about you . . . who loves you in spite of your fears . . . in spite of your failings and your doubts . . .

○ The dark clouds begin to break, and you see the one carrying you for the first time . . . and you understand why you did not fall . . . why you did not perish along with the creature of fear and doubt. . . . You did not fall because you trusted in God . . . you did not abandon your faith or your beliefs . . . in that split second of decision, you chose God . . . and God did not abandon you. . . . You are resting in the palm of his hand . . .

○ Now become aware of your breathing . . . and your presence in this room . . . in this moment. . . . Slowly open your eyes and breathe deeply in . . . and out . . .

Step 4: Individual Reflection
and Small-Group Faith Sharing

Ask everyone to return to their small group. Distribute paper and pens or pencils. Once everyone is settled, continue with these or similar words:

○ Spend a few moments thinking about the images from the meditation that speak most powerfully to you.

○ If you wish, draw or jot down some thoughts about these images. In a couple of minutes, you will be invited to share an image or reflection with the small group.

Continue by inviting the participants to share in their small groups, using the mutual invitation process. Ask them to share an image or thought from the meditation and to briefly discuss its meaning and significance.

Note: If the participants are unfamiliar with the mutual invitation process, take a minute to summarize the description on page 10 (see "Using the Mutual Invitation Process to Share Faith" in the introduction). Be sure to remind them of the option to pass.

Step 5: Conclusion and Closing Prayer

Continue with these or similar words:

○ We will now hear the proclamation of a passage from Psalm 40.

○ As you listen, think about the hand of God holding, guiding, and protecting you in the coming week. Think about the trust that is necessary for you to be open to God's will for your life.

Invite the designated reader to proclaim Psalm 40:2–9.

After the reading, invite the group to join hands while you say the following prayer:

○ Feel the power of the hands that connect us to one another. The power that says you are not alone. Now feel the presence of the hand of God uniting each of us to one another and ultimately to himself. As we rest in the hand of God.

Conclude by inviting everyone to pray the Lord's Prayer.

Part Three

Faith Sharing with Media Messages

Media Messages and Faith Sharing

Young people have an insatiable appetite for the media. They "consume" large quantities at increasingly faster rates. Today's teens are quick reads—plugged in, tuned in, visually adept, and fully wired. They exist in a media-based culture that permeates all facets of their lives, including their language and beliefs. For this reason, a section of *FaithSharing* is dedicated to helping teens use the media for reflecting on and sharing their faith. This section draws on various aspects of the media (songs, movies, television programs, billboards, and magazines) and combines them with Scripture and reflection to help young people step back and recognize the presence of God in the here and now.

A Note About Using Handouts

The handouts for the activities in part 3 include the titles of songs, television programs, and movies. This information can become outdated quickly. Therefore, the titles listed are from several decades, so that none of the handouts is limited to one particular time period. You may invite participants to add recent titles to the handouts to personalize and update them.

Media Messages 1
Sing a New Song

Scripture: Psalm 33:3–5,20–22

Overview

The Book of Psalms served as a popular playlist of songs for the Israelites, who sang to God to express their joys, struggles, and fears. This faith-sharing experience invites participants to reflect on how one might use popular songs of today to connect and communicate with God.

Estimated Time: 10–15 minutes

Preparation Steps

- Gather the following items:
  - ☐ pens or pencils, one for each participant
  - ☐ copies of handout 1–A, "God's Playlist," one for each participant
  - ☐ *The Catholic Youth Bible* or another Bible
- Mark the Scripture reading (Psalm 33:3–5,20–22) in a Bible and select a reader to proclaim it during step 3.

Procedure

Step 1: Creation of Faith-Sharing Groups

If the group size is larger than ten, divide into small faith-sharing groups of five to seven. Select one person in each faith-sharing group to serve as the prayer leader.

Step 2: Focus the Group

Begin the faith-sharing process with these or similar words:

- Song lyrics often seem to express what simple words cannot. Somehow, songs take us deeper than words alone. Whether we are sad, mad, or glad, songs express the breadth and depth of our emotions.
- The Book of Psalms served as a popular playlist of songs for the Israelites, who would sing to God to express their joys, struggles, and fears.

Step 3: Scripture Proclamation

Invite everyone to listen to part of Psalm 33, which expresses gladness and thanksgiving. Ask the participants to imagine what the psalmist may have been feeling when he wrote these lyrics to sing to God. Signal the designated reader to proclaim Psalm 33:3–5, 20–22.

Step 4: Playlist Reflection

Distribute pens or pencils and a copy of handout 1–A, "God's Playlist," to each participant. Review the instructions on the handout. Invite everyone to jot down their thoughts on the handout as they work. Allow several minutes for this task.

Step 5: Faith Sharing

Invite the participants to begin sharing their reflections with these or similar words:

- I now invite the prayer leader for each group to lead the group in a few minutes of sharing. Please identify the two songs you chose and explain the meaning behind your choices. Please take turns using the mutual invitation process.

Note: If the participants are unfamiliar with the mutual invitation process, take a minute to summarize the description on page 10 (see "Using the Mutual Invitation Process to Share Faith" in the introduction). Be sure to remind them of the option to pass.

Step 6: Conclusion and Closing Prayer

Conclude by inviting each participant to review the playlist again and select a song title that reflects the message they will try to sing back to God through their actions during the coming week. After a minute or two, invite each person, if he or she wishes, to say aloud the name of the song he or she selected, using the phrase, "The song I hope to sing to God this week is . . ."

Note: If the group is large, ask the participants to do this sharing in small groups. Then, when you call everyone together for the concluding prayer, begin by asking a few volunteers to share the song title that reflects what they hope to sing to God.

Close with the following prayer:

God of the song,
Help us to open our hearts and souls to your melody this week.
Gift us with the voice to sing of your goodness and steadfast love.
Transform us into a living choir of angels who will sing to the world a
    new song of faith, hope, and love.
Amen.

God's Playlist

1. Review the song titles listed below. Focus your attention on the words in the titles rather than on the lyrics.

2. Identify the song title that best reflects the message God is trying to sing to you this week.

3. Identify the song title that best reflects the message you want God to sing to a friend or family member who is on your mind this week.

4. Reflect on the meanings of your selected song titles and think about why you chose them.

"All Shook Up"
(Elvis Presley)

"Bridge over Troubled Water"
(Simon and Garfunkel)

"Dream On"
(Aerosmith)

"Every Breath You Take"
(The Police)

"Gloria"
(Them)

"God Only Knows"
(The Beach Boys)

"Good Vibrations"
(The Beach Boys)

"I Got You (I Feel Good)"
(James Brown)

"I Want to Hold Your Hand"
(The Beatles)

"Johnny B. Goode"
(Chuck Berry)

"Let It Be"
(Beatles)

"Let's Stay Together"
(Al Green)

"Living on a Prayer"
(Bon Jovi)

"Respect"
(Aretha Franklin)

"Stairway to Heaven"
(Led Zeppelin)

"Stand by Me"
(Ben E. King)

"Stayin' Alive"
(Bee Gees)

"Walk This Way"
(Aerosmith)

"We've Only Just Begun"
(The Carpenters)

"What's Going On?"
(Marvin Gaye)

"Whole Lotta Love"
(Led Zeppelin)

"You Are the Sunshine of My Life"
(Stevie Wonder)

"You Really Got Me"
(Kinks)

"Your Song"
(Elton John)

Media Messages 2
TV Guide

Scripture: Psalm 139:1–16,23–24

Overview

Whether for good or bad, television has become the focal point of and gathering place for many families. From cartoons to reality shows, soap operas to classics, the young generation both identifies with and seeks comfort in what is shown on television. This faith-sharing session is intended to help participants find connections between our media culture and our God, and to recognize that God sees everything, including the deepest needs and hungers of our hearts.

Estimated Time: 15–20 minutes

Preparation Steps

- Gather the following items:
  - ☐ pens or pencils, one for each participant
  - ☐ copies of handout 2–A, "Prime-Time TV Guide," one for each participant
  - ☐ THE CATHOLIC YOUTH BIBLE or another Bible
- Mark the Scripture reading (Psalm 139:1–16,23–24) in a Bible and select a reader to proclaim it during step 5.

Procedure

Step 1: Creation of Faith-Sharing Groups

If the group size is larger than ten, divide into small faith-sharing groups of five to seven. Select one person in each faith-sharing group to serve as the prayer leader.

Step 2: Focus the Group

Begin the faith-sharing process with these or similar words:
- ○ Think about how powerful television is in our culture. Certainly, it determines many people's schedules, for example, when we wake and sleep, when we entertain company, and when we just want to escape from the world.
- ○ Today we will use TV shows to help us look at our lives, our faith, and the journey we are taking.

Step 3: Select and Meditate on the TV Guide

Distribute pens or pencils and handout 2–A, "Prime-Time TV Guide," and provide the following directions:
- ○ For each question, select a TV show from the list that best answers that question for you this month.
- ○ Please focus on the meaning of the title as it appears and do not dwell on the content of the show itself.
- ○ After you have made your selections, spend a moment reflecting silently on why you made these choices and jot down your thoughts on your handout.

Step 4: Sharing Reflections

Invite the participants to begin sharing their reflections with these or similar words:
- ○ I now invite the prayer leader for each group to lead the group in a few minutes of sharing. Taking one question at a time, the prayer leader should begin sharing the choice she or he made and the meaning behind the choice and then invite others to share their choices and reasons, if they wish. After all have had a chance to share, move to the next question, until all five have been covered.

Allow several minutes for this sharing.

Step 5: Conclusion and Closing Prayer

Conclude with these or similar words:
- ○ Thousands of years ago, BTV (before TV), the psalmist considered how ever-present and powerful God was in a person's life. As we conclude our faith-sharing session, listen to the psalm proclaimed as you imagine all that fills God's TV screen.

Invite the designated reader to proclaim Psalm 139:1–16,23–24.

Invite the young people to offer, in prayer, one image or word that describes God. Ask them to use the phrase, "God is _____." For example, "God is everywhere" or "God is love" or "God is Creator."

Conclude with the following brief prayer:
- ○ For all that God is, we give thanks. Amen.

Prime–Time TV Guide

My Top Five Selections

Which show best describes your life right now?

_____

Which show best describes your family life right now?

_____

Which show best describes your faith life right now?

_____

Which show best describes your personal growth over the past year?

_____

Which show best describes your hope for the coming months?

_____

Network	7:00	8:00	9:00	10:00	11:00
Fav TV	Friends	Hope & Faith	Lost	Saturday Night Live	Will & Grace
Toon Time	The Flash	The Joker	Pokemon	Superman	Wonder Woman
The Soap Dish	As the World Turns	The Bold & the Beautiful	Days of Our Lives	The Guiding Light	The Young & the Restless
Game Show Network	Family Feud	Jeopardy	Let's Make a Deal	The Price Is Right	Wheel of Fortune
Reality TV	The Apprentice	Big Brother	Extreme Make-over	Funniest Home Videos	Survivor
The Classic Channel	All in the Family	Good Times	Happy Days	Highway to Heaven	Touched by an Angel

Media Messages 3
At the Movies

Scripture: Exodus 3:1–10

Overview

Good filmmakers use images and emotions to reach us and communicate deep thoughts and feelings. During this faith-sharing experience, participants will be asked to reflect on several aspects of their lives. They will use movies and movie titles to help draw attention to some of the deeper issues and hopes that characterize their lives.

Estimated Time: 20 minutes

Preparation Steps

- Gather the following items:
  - ☐ pens or pencils, one for each participant
  - ☐ copies of handout 3–A, "Now Playing at My Cinema 6," one for each participant
  - ☐ THE CATHOLIC YOUTH BIBLE or another Bible
- Mark the Scripture reading (Exodus 3:1–10) in a Bible and select a reader to proclaim it during step 5.

Procedure

Step 1: Creation of Faith-Sharing Groups

If the group size is larger than ten, divide into small faith-sharing groups of five to seven. Select one person in each faith-sharing group to serve as the prayer leader.

Step 2: Focus the Group

Begin the faith-sharing process with these or similar words:

- Simply put, film moves us. The images and emotions contained in a good film can leave an imprint deep within us.
- Often a good film will remind us of a struggle, an emotion, a situation, or a dream that we have.
- During this faith-sharing experience, you will be invited to use movies and titles to try to illustrate some of the hopes, struggles, and issues that are part of your life at the moment, including your relationship with God.

Step 3: Movie List Reflection

Distribute pens or pencils and a copy of handout 3–A, "Now Playing at My Cinema 6," to each participant.

- On your cinema page is a marquee with six openings. Each opening corresponds to a question. Please review the list of movies on your handout and write an answer to each question in the corresponding marquee. You may add a movie title not on the list, if you wish. Your response can reflect just the meaning of the title itself or some other meaning the movie has for you.
- After you make your selections, spend a few moments reflecting silently on why you made these choices and jot down your thoughts on your paper.

Step 4: Sharing Reflections

Invite the participants to begin sharing their reflections with these or similar words:

- I now invite the prayer leader for each group to lead the group in a few minutes of sharing. Take one question at a time. Share your answers and explain your choice of movie title and whether your choice is based solely on the title or has to do with the meaning of the actual movie. The prayer leader should go first and then invite others who wish to share to do so.

Step 5: Conclusion and Closing Prayer

Conclude with these or similar words:

- Film is designed to get our attention. Sometimes it even makes us step back and see something differently. A few thousand years ago, Moses had a similar type of encounter, not with a movie but with a burning bush. It was a sight that changed his life and connected him personally with a living, present, and caring God. As you listen to this reading, think about what image God may be placing along your path to catch your attention and bring about a change in you.

Invite the designated reader to proclaim Exodus 3:1–10.

Close with the following prayer:

o   Lord God, gift us with the eyes to see you at work in the world and in our lives. Help us to notice the Christ in each person we meet and to see the signs of your love and presence that you place before us each day. We ask this through Christ our Lord. Amen.

Now Playing at My Cinema 6

1.
2.
3.
4.
5.
6.

Screen 1: Which movie or title best describes your character or personality?

Screen 2: Which movie or title best describes your biggest struggle right now?

Screen 3: Which movie or title best describes a life dream or goal of yours?

Screen 4: Which movie or title best describes the direction in which your life is headed?

Screen 5: Which movie or title best describes your deepest hope or longing?

Screen 6: Which movie or title best describes your relationship with God right now?

Alien
Almost Famous
Back to the Future
A Beautiful Mind
The Best Years of Our Lives
Big
Breaking Away
Brief Encounter
Bringing Up Baby
A Bug's Life
Cast Away
Catch Me If You Can
Clear and Present Danger
Contact
Daredevil
The Day the Earth Stood Still
Days of Heaven
Deep Impact
Field of Dreams
Finding Nemo
Finding Neverland
From Here to Eternity

Funny Girl
Ghost
Glory
Gone with the Wind
The Graduate
Greed
Home Alone
The Hustler
In the Heat of the Night
The Incredibles
Independence Day
It Happened One Night
It's a Mad, Mad, Mad, Mad
    World
It's a Wonderful Life
Jesus Christ Superstar
Liar, Liar
The Longest Day
Look Who's Talking
Lord of the Rings
Love Story
Mask

Men in Black
Million Dollar Baby
Minority Report
Mission Impossible
My Fair Lady
Napoleon Dynamite
Notorious
Oh, God!
Phenomenon
A Place in the Sun
Rear Window
Rebel Without a Cause
The Searchers
Shadow of a Doubt
Singin' in the Rain
Some Like It Hot
Something's Gotta Give
The Sound of Music
Star Wars
The Ten Commandments
Touch of Evil
War and Peace

Media Messages 4
On the Cover

Scripture: Luke 4:14–21

Overview

Magazine covers are designed to attract readers, enticing them, through provocative graphics and headlines, to open up the magazine and discover its content. This experience invites each young person to imagine her or his life as the subject of a magazine. What would it be called? What cover shot might appear? What "provocative" issues would be headlining the cover? And what page would feature a story pertaining to her or his faith?

Estimated Time: 20–25 minutes

Preparation Steps

- Gather the following items:
  - ☐ pens or pencils, one for each participant
  - ☐ markers, several for each participant
  - ☐ copies of handout 4–A, "Covered," one for each participant
  - ☐ copies of handout 4–B, "Cover Shots," one for each participant
  - ☐ THE CATHOLIC YOUTH BIBLE or another Bible
  - ☐ CD of instrumental music (optional)
- Mark the Scripture reading (Luke 4:14–21) in a Bible and select a reader to proclaim it during step 5.

Procedure

Step 1: Creation of Faith-Sharing Groups

If the group size is larger than ten, divide into small faith-sharing groups of five to seven. Select one person in each faith-sharing group to serve as the prayer leader.

Step 2: Focus the Group

Begin the faith-sharing process with these or similar words:

- Magazine covers are designed to attract readers, enticing them, through provocative graphics and headlines, to open up the magazine and discover its content.
- This experience invites you to imagine your life as the subject of a magazine. What would it be called? What cover shot might appear? What "provocative" issues would be headlining the cover? On which page would your faith appear?
- Today's faith-sharing experience will give us time to think about these questions as we prepare the covers for our own magazines.

Step 3: Creation of Magazine Covers

Distribute pens or pencils, markers, and a copy of handout 4–A, "Covered," and handout 4–B, "Cover Shots," to each participant. Provide the following directions:

- Think about your life right now and select an image from handout 4–B that represents something significant occurring in your life now. Then fill in each of the areas on handout 4–A as indicated. After you have completed all the cover components, feel free to decorate your cover as much as you would like. You will have 5 to 10 minutes to work on this quietly before sharing.

You may wish to play a song or reflective music during this time.

Step 4: Sharing Reflections

Invite the participants to begin sharing their reflections with these or similar words:

- I now invite the prayer leader for each group to lead the group in several minutes of sharing. Please share your magazine covers and explain the meaning behind each section. Please take turns using the mutual invitation process.
- After everyone has shared, take a few minutes to try to answer each others' questions about faith, listed in box 4.

Note: If the participants are unfamiliar with the mutual invitation process, take a minute to summarize the description on page 10 (see "Using the Mutual Invitation Process to Share Faith" in the introduction). Be sure to remind them of the option to pass.

Allow 10 to 15 minutes for this sharing.

Step 5: Conclusion and Closing Prayer

Conclude with these or similar words:
- ○ Let us conclude our faith sharing by listening to a reading from Luke's Gospel.
- ○ Jesus was just returning from forty days in the desert, where he was tempted by Satan to base his life on fame, fortune, and comfort. In rejecting those headlines (and Satan), he instead chose a different, and far more difficult, road.
- ○ Listen to what Jesus says about the basis for his life and ministry in the future, and imagine the headlines that might appear on his magazine cover as a result.

Invite the designated reader to proclaim Luke 4:14–21. After the reading, invite the young people to think about what God is asking each of them to proclaim through their lives this week. After a moment, invite them to share their own prayer proclamations by using the phrase, "Lord help me to proclaim . . ."

For each petition, invite the participants to respond, "Spirit of the Lord, hear us."

Conclude with the following prayer:
- ○ Dear Lord,
  Help us to withstand the pressure to be someone other than who you created us to be. Let the headlines proclaimed by our lives give witness to all of who we are and whose we are. We ask this through Christ our Lord. Amen.

Covered

Complete the boxes in the order in which they are numbered.

2. My Magazine . . .

Create a title for your magazine here, based on the image you have selected in box 1.

1. Cover Pic . . .

Draw or copy the image you chose from handout 4–B to represent your life right now.

3. Inside This Month . . .

List three to five events, or "stories," that are unfolding in your life right now and the page numbers on which they are found in the magazine (with page 1 being most important and page 100 being the last, or least important, page).

4. The Big Question . . .

List a faith question you have been struggling with recently.

5. Coming Soon . . .

Give a title to a major event or decision that is coming up in the next few months.

Cover Shots

Media Messages 5
Signs of Strength

Scripture: Luke 2:8–14

Overview

In 1998, an anonymous donor in Texas asked an advertising company to develop a few simple sayings "from God" and place them on billboards around the city. These simple but profound phrases (such as "Follow me" and "Tell the kids I love them") soon appeared on billboards throughout the country. They led to the creation of the GodSpeaks Web site and a second ad campaign in 2005. This faith-sharing experience is designed to invite young people to reflect on the following related questions: What might God place on a billboard to get your attention? What would you like others to see and hear from God?

Estimated Time: 15 minutes

Preparation Steps

- Gather the following items:
  - ☐ pens or pencils, one for each participant
  - ☐ markers, several for each participant
  - ☐ copies of handout 5–A, "Signs of the Times," one for each participant
  - ☐ THE CATHOLIC YOUTH BIBLE or another Bible
- Mark the Scripture reading (Luke 2:8–14) in a Bible and select a reader to proclaim it during step 5.
- To read about the GodSpeaks ad campaign and to view the billboards referred to in the overview, go to the GodSpeaks Web site.

Procedure

Step 1: Creation of Faith-Sharing Groups

If the group size is larger than ten people, divide into small faith-sharing groups of five to seven. Select one person in each faith-sharing group to serve as the prayer leader.

Step 2: Focus the Group

Begin the faith-sharing process with these or similar words:
- In 1998, an anonymous donor in Texas asked an advertising company to develop a few simple sayings "from God" and put them on billboards around the city. These simple but profound phrases (such as "Follow me" and "Tell the kids I love them") soon appeared throughout the country. Eventually, they even spawned a Web site and another ad campaign in 2005.
- This faith-sharing experience invites each of you to consider two related questions: What might God place on a billboard to get your attention? What would you like others to see and hear from God?

Step 3: Create the Billboards

Distribute pens or pencils, markers, and handout 5–A, "Signs of the Times," and provide the following directions:
- On your paper are two blank billboards.
- The first one is labeled "internal billboard." Please use it to write a short phrase that God might be trying to say to you to get your attention or remind you of something you need to hear from God on a daily basis.
- The second billboard is labeled "external billboard." Please use this one to write a short phrase that you want God to communicate to another person or group of people. Below the billboard, indicate where you would place this billboard to achieve maximum coverage of the message you want communicated by God.
- Then spend a few moments reflecting silently on why you made these choices and jot down your thoughts on your paper.

Step 4: Sharing Reflections

Invite the participants to begin sharing their reflections with these or similar words:
- I now invite the prayer leader for each group to lead the group in several minutes of sharing. Please share your billboards and explain

the meanings behind your choices. Please take turns using the mutual invitation process.

Note: If the participants are unfamiliar with the mutual invitation process, take a minute to summarize the description on page 10 (see "Using the Mutual Invitation Process to Share Faith" in the introduction). Be sure to remind them of the option to pass.

Step 5: Conclusion and Closing Prayer

Conclude with these or similar words:
- Let us conclude our faith sharing by listening to the proclamation of a story from the Gospel of Luke. It tells about one of the most famous signs used in Scripture, one that showed God's immense and personal love for God's people.
- As you listen to it, imagine what message might have appeared on a billboard if there had been one next to the stable that night.

Invite the designated reader to proclaim Luke 2:8–14.
Lead the young people in the following prayer:
- God of sign and wonder,
  Walk with us as we seek your message and the meaning that holds for each of us. This week, let us become living signs of your love and mercy to the world. We ask this through Christ our Lord. Amen.

Signs of the Times

Internal Billboard

This billboard appears inside your home where only you can see it and where you will pass it several times each day. Use it to write a short saying that God wants to speak to you to get your attention or remind you of something you need to hear on a daily basis.

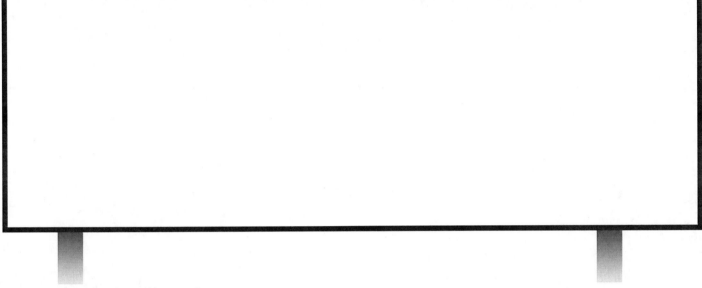

External Billboard

This billboard can appear anywhere in the world. Use it to write a short saying that you want God to communicate to another person or group of people. Below the billboard, indicate the group or person to whom it is directed and where you would place the billboard to achieve maximum coverage of the message you want communicated by God. Be prepared to discuss why you chose this particular person or group to see this message.

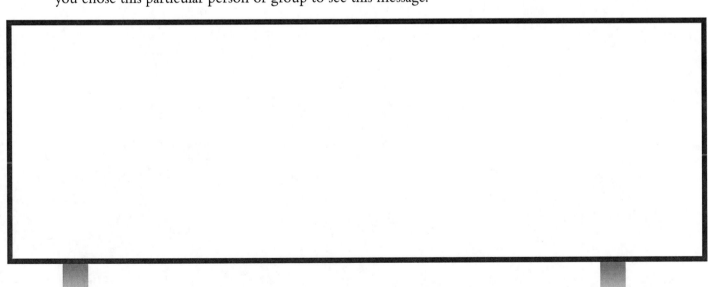

Part Four

Faith Sharing with Objects and Images

What Is Faith Sharing with Objects and Images?

This section of *FaithSharing* uses various objects and images to help young people connect faith with life. Attending to objects and images allows young people to enter the world of symbol and metaphor and take their journey to a deeper level of awareness and meaning. Because the experience of God's presence and grace in our lives goes far beyond what words alone can describe, symbols and metaphors can be helpful tools for faith sharing. The visual and kinesthetic learners in the group will enjoy the opportunity to move beyond words into the multidimensional sphere of symbolic thought processing. Perhaps most important, using everyday objects and images to explore a particular experience of faith is both an engaging and a nonthreatening exercise for faith sharing and reflection. The leader may find that a number of participants who were hesitant to share their faith previously will engage in faith sharing with objects and images.

Some of the objects needed in this section must be gathered ahead of time, but all are easy to find. The images needed are provided on the resource page connected to each session. Leaders have the option of individualizing the images by creating separate posters for each object, which can be hung around the room or placed on the floor for all to see.

Objects and Images 1
Signs of the Times

Scripture: Matthew 16:1–3

Overview

This faith-sharing experience uses the many images and meanings of signs to invite participants to consider the road on which they are traveling and the signs that God may be placing before them as they journey along the way.

Estimated Time: 15–20 minutes

Preparation Steps

- Gather the following items:
  - ☐ pens or pencils, one for each participant
  - ☐ copies of handout 1–A, "Signs Along the Way," one for each participant
  - ☐ THE CATHOLIC YOUTH BIBLE or another Bible
- Mark the Scripture reading (Matthew 16:1–3) in a Bible and designate a reader to proclaim it during step 3.
- Create individual signs and place them along a portion of the wall or on the floor where everyone can see them (optional).

Procedure

Step 1: Creation of Faith-Sharing Groups

If the group size is larger than ten, divide into small faith-sharing groups of five to seven. Select one person in each faith-sharing group to serve as the prayer leader.

Step 2: Focus the Group

Begin the faith-sharing process with these or similar words:

- Before we are allowed to drive, we must be able to interpret many different road signs. If we do not know what the signs mean and what they require of us, we may end up in the wrong place, headed in the wrong direction, or, worse, off the road entirely.
- Today, our faith sharing invites us to consider the road each of us is on and the signs that God may be placing before each of us.

Step 3: Proclamation of Scripture

Begin the proclamation of Scripture with these or similar words:

- The Scriptures have many stories in which Jesus performs signs and wonders. In Jesus's time, not everyone grasped the meaning of these events, however. Many simply lacked the faith to recognize and believe what they were witnessing. Listen to one response Jesus gives to those who "demanded a sign" that he was the messiah.

Invite the designated reader to proclaim Matthew 16:1–3.

- Just as Jesus challenged the Pharisees and Sadducees to see and interpret the signs that were in front of them, this faith-sharing experience invites each of you to look closely for the signs that God may be placing along your journey of faith this week.

Step 4: Select and Meditate on the Signs

Distribute a pen or pencil and a copy of handout 1–A, "Signs Along the Way," to each participant. Provide the following directions:

- Look over the images of the many signs and select two that God is placing before you now in your life.
- Meditate on what these choices mean for you in relation to the road on which you are traveling. Jot down your thoughts near the images.

Allow a few minutes of quiet reflection for this step.

Step 5: Sharing Reflections

Invite the participants to share their two chosen images and the meaning behind the choices in their small groups. Ask them to use the mutual invitation process.

Note: If the participants are unfamiliar with this process, take a minute to summarize the description on page 10 (see "Using the Mutual Invitation Process to Share Faith" in the introduction). Be sure to remind them of the option to pass.

Allow several minutes for this sharing.

Step 6: Conclusion and Closing Prayer

Conclude with these or similar words:

○ God is present to us now and throughout our life's journey. Our challenge is to look with eyes of faith to see the signs of God's presence.

Introduce a closing prayer:

○ Let us conclude this time of faith sharing by offering a prayer aloud for a concern, a hope, or an intention that is occupying our thoughts at this moment.

○ Our response to each prayer is, "Lord, show us the way."

Conclude with the following prayer:

○ Lord of signs and wonders,
Gift us with the eyes of faith to see your hand at work in the world and within our lives. Steer us in the direction that we need to walk this week so that we stay on course in our journey of faith. Amen.

Signs Along the Way

Look over the many signs and select two that God is placing before you now in your life. Meditate on what these choices mean for you in relation to the road on which you are traveling. Jot down your thoughts near the images.

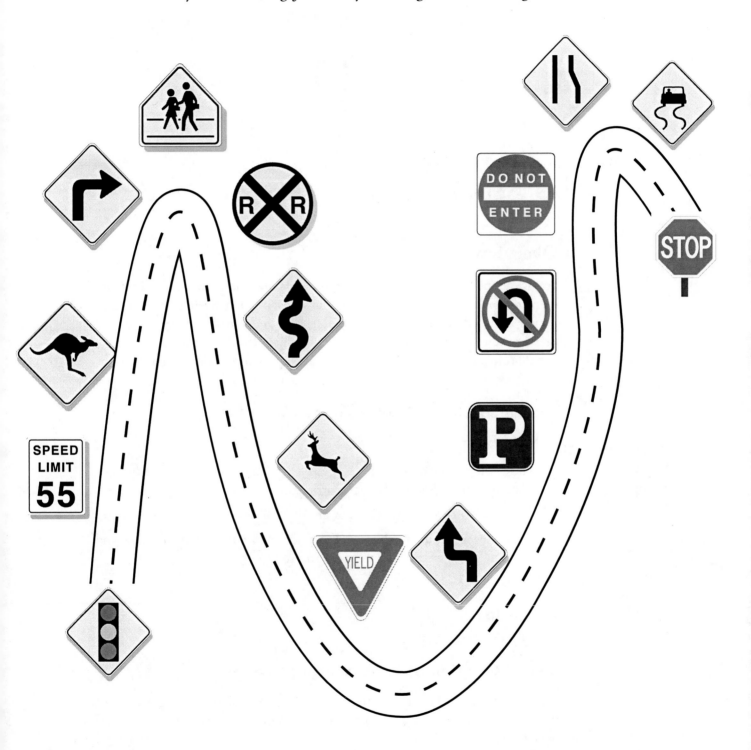

Objects and Images 2
Many Objects, One Faith

Scripture: 1 Corinthians 12:12–19

Overview

Young people often wonder what their gifts are and how they might use them to make a difference. In this faith-sharing experience, each young person is asked to select an object that will help lead the group toward sharing their faith with one another. This is proof that even the most unusual or insignificant contribution may hold the key to another's journey of faith.

Estimated Time: 15–20 minutes

Preparation Steps

- Gather the following items:
  - ☐ pens or pencils, one for each participant
  - ☐ THE CATHOLIC YOUTH BIBLE or another Bible
- Mark the Scripture reading (1 Corinthians 12:12–19) in a Bible and designate a reader to proclaim it during step 5.

Procedure

Step 1: Creation of Faith-Sharing Groups

If the group size is larger than ten, divide into small faith-sharing groups of five to seven. Select one person in each faith-sharing group to serve as the prayer leader.

Step 2: Focus the Group

Begin the faith-sharing process with these or similar words:
- We often wonder what is unique or special about us, what our gifts are, and how we might end up using them to make a difference in the world. Often, the gifts for which we are so desperately looking are already within us, being used on a daily basis, but we are not aware of the difference they may be making in another's life.
- To demonstrate this, each of you will be asked to select an object that will help lead the group toward sharing their faith with one another. This activity will show us that even the most unusual or insignificant contribution may hold the key to another's journey of faith.

Step 3: Selection of Objects and Meditation

Invite the participants to place one object that they have with them in the center of the group. Provide some examples, such as something from a wallet, purse, or pocket, or a piece of jewelry or other accessory. Ask them to take turns placing their items in the center, and challenge them not to choose an item that someone else has already placed in the center.

Continue with these or similar words:
- Everyone is invited to select an object that symbolically speaks to a current life situation that is on your mind right now, and spend a minute or so reflecting on the connection that your faith has with that event or situation. An object may be selected by more than one person in a small group; therefore, once an individual has shared his or her response to an object, the object should be placed in the middle of the group so others can refer to it.

Step 4: Sharing Reflections

Invite the participants to begin sharing their reflections with these or similar words:
- I now invite the prayer leader of each group to share the object she or he has chosen, as well as the meaning of the event it symbolizes and the way she or he believes God is connected to all of this. Please take turns using the mutual invitation process.

Note: If the participants are unfamiliar with the mutual invitation process, take a minute to summarize the description on page 10 (see "Using the Mutual Invitation Process to Share Faith" in the introduction). Be sure to remind them of the option to pass.

Step 5: Conclusion and Closing Prayer

Conclude with these or similar words:

- The Apostle Paul used the image of the body to help the early Christians in the town of Corinth understand that each person has been blessed with special gifts and each is a vital part of the spiritual Body of Christ.

- To deny or discount any part of that spiritual body is to deny our very selves and our own identity as Christians. Just as each of you made a contribution toward this faith-sharing experience, God is asking each of you to be an integral part of the Body of Christ.

- Let us conclude our faith sharing by listening to Paul's words from the First Letter to the Corinthians.

Invite the designated reader to proclaim 1 Corinthians 12:12–19.

Conclude by inviting everyone to join together in prayer:

- As one body in Christ, let us join hands and pray together the Lord's Prayer.

Objects and Images 3
Forecasting Faith

Scripture: Luke 8:22–25

Overview

If there is one thing we have in common with those around us, it is the weather. This probably explains why the weather is one of the most common topics of conversation. In this session, the young people will be invited to use the weather as a way to reflect on their lives and to gauge their faith journey.

Estimated Time: 15–20 minutes

Preparation Steps

- Gather the following items:
  - ☐ pens or pencils, one for each participant
  - ☐ copies of handout 3–A, "Faith Forecast," one for each participant
- Mark the Scripture reading (Luke 8:22–25) and designate a reader to proclaim it during step 5.

Procedure

Step 1: Creation of Faith-Sharing Groups

If the group size is larger than ten, divide into small faith-sharing groups of five to seven. Select one person in each faith-sharing group to serve as the prayer leader.

Step 2: Focus the Group

Begin the faith-sharing process with these or similar words:

- ○ If there's one thing we have in common with those around us, it is the weather. This probably explains why it is one of the most common topics of conversation. It also serves as a way for us to reflect on our lives and gauge our faith journey. That is exactly what we will do in this faith-sharing experience.

Step 3: Create the Weather Forecast

Distribute pens or pencils and a copy of handout 3–A, "Faith Forecast," to each participant. Provide the following directions:

- ○ Think about how your life's journey is going right now, and use the weather signs and gauges on the handout to complete the forecasts and readings for the different areas indicated. Note that the "record high" and "record low" refer to the best and worst times in your life thus far.

Step 4: Sharing Reflections

Invite the participants to begin sharing their reflections with these or similar words:

- ○ I now invite the prayer leader for each group to share his or her weather forecast as well as the meaning behind his or her choices. Please take turns in your small groups, using the mutual invitation process.

Note: If the participants are unfamiliar with the mutual invitation process, take a minute to summarize the description on page 10 (see "Using the Mutual Invitation Process to Share Faith" in the introduction). Be sure to remind them of the option to pass.

Allow several minutes for this sharing.

Step 5: Conclusion and Closing Prayer

Conclude with these or similar words:

- ○ Weather was a big concern in Jesus's time, even more so than today because there was less protection from it, especially if you were at sea. In this reading, the weather turns from bad to worse and then to, well, perfect.
- ○ As you listen to this reading, think about the storms in your life and what Jesus may be able to do with them.

Invite the designated reader to proclaim Luke 8:22–25.

Invite the young people to offer a prayer petition using the phrase, "Lord, help see me through the storm of _____."

Close with this prayer:

○ Lord, lead us through the storms that surround and paralyze us with fear. Help us to see you as the calming force amidst all our concerns so that we turn to you with trust and hope. We ask this through Jesus Christ, who controls the wind and the sea. Amen.

Faith Forecast

Reflect on your life right now, and use the weather signs and gauges to complete the forecasts and readings for the different areas indicated.

Last week's conditions were: ☐

due to _____

The coming week is expected to be: ☐

due to _____

Today's Friendship Factor
(how strong your friendships are right now)

Strong 100
90
80
70
60
50
40
30
20
10
Critical 0

Today's Faith Index
(how close I feel to God today)

Strong 100
90
80
70
60
50
40
30
20
10
Critical 0

Weather Almanac:

My record high was set in _____

due to _____

My record low was set in _____

because _____

Objects and Images 4
Rock of Ages

Scripture: Psalm 31:1–9

Overview

The image of a rock is often used in Scripture to refer to God, especially in the Old Testament. This experience invites participants to reflect on the type of rock they need to steady their lives right now so they can discover for themselves that God rocks!

Estimated Time: 15–20 minutes

Preparation Steps

- Gather the following items:
    - ☐ pens or pencils, one for each participant
    - ☐ copies of handout 4–A, "Rock of Ages," one for each participant
    - ☐ THE CATHOLIC YOUTH BIBLE or another Bible
- Mark the Scripture reading (Psalm 31:1–9) in a Bible and select a reader to proclaim it during step 3.

Note: Instead of using the handout, you can display rocks of different shapes and sizes where everyone can see them.

Procedure

Step 1: Creation of Faith-Sharing Groups

If the group size is larger than ten, divide into small faith-sharing groups of five to seven. Select one person in each faith-sharing group to serve as the prayer leader.

Step 2: Focus the Group

Begin the faith-sharing process with these or similar words:
- Like a rock, God is steadfast. Like a rock, God is strong. Like a rock, God is. The image of a rock is used many times in Scripture to refer to God, especially in the Old Testament.
- What type of rock do you need God to be for you this week? A mountain to remind you of his presence? A cave where you can seek shelter? A boulder that will hold you in place, or perhaps the smallest of pebbles that you can carry around at all times?

Step 3: Proclamation of Scripture

Introduce the proclamation of Scripture with these or similar words:
- Listen to a reading from the Book of Psalms recounting a prayer of hope for deliverance from difficult times. As you listen, think about some of the difficult times you have experienced recently.

Invite the designated reader to proclaim Psalm 31:1–9.

Step 4: Selection of Rocks and Meditation

Distribute pens or pencils and a copy of handout 4–A, "Rock of Ages," to each participant. Provide the following directions:
- Look over the images of rocks on your paper and think about your life right now. Select the rock that will best serve as a reminder of God's steadfast presence in this coming week. Then spend a minute or so reflecting on your choice. Jot down some thoughts, if you wish.

Step 5: Sharing Reflections

Invite the participants to begin sharing their reflections with these or similar words:
- I now invite the prayer leader for each group to begin sharing the rock image she or he chose as well as the meaning behind the choice.

Please take turns in your small groups, using the mutual invitation process.

Note: If the participants are unfamiliar with the mutual invitation process, take a minute to summarize the description on page 10 (see "Using the Mutual Invitation Process to Share Faith" in the introduction). Be sure to remind them of the option to pass.

Allow several minutes for this sharing.

Step 6: Conclusion and Closing Prayer

Conclude with these or similar words:
- As we end our faith-sharing time together, let us offer a prayer of petition to God. The petition should have the word *rock* in it, for example, "Lord, be my rock this week" or "God, my life is rocky right now; please be with me."
- Let our response to each petition be, "Lord, you rock!"

Close with the following prayer:
- Lord you are our rock and refuge, especially in the tough times. Help us to see your steady presence at work in our lives this week. In Jesus's name we pray. Amen.

Rock of Ages

Think about a difficult struggle in your life right now, and select the rock image that most powerfully signifies God's presence with you. Jot down your thoughts about what you need from God at this moment.

Objects and Images 5
Seeds Scattered and Sown

Scripture: Mark 4:3–9

Overview

The parable of the sower provides us with excellent images with which to examine and share our faith. In this session, young people will be invited to apply the parable to their own faith life.

Estimated Time: 15–20 minutes

Preparation Steps

- Gather the following items:
    - ☐ pens or pencils, one for each participant
    - ☐ copies of handout 5–A, "Scattered Seeds," one for each participant
    - ☐ THE CATHOLIC YOUTH BIBLE or another Bible
- Mark the Scripture reading (Mark 4:3–9) in a Bible and select a reader to proclaim it during step 3.

Note: In lieu of the handout, you can display rocks, weeds, seeds, soil, and images of birds on the floor, where all can gather around. Use the scenes on the handout to plan the display.

Procedure

Step 1: Creation of Faith-Sharing Groups

If the group size is larger than ten, divide into small faith-sharing groups of five to seven. Select one person in each faith-sharing group to serve as the prayer leader.

Step 2: Focus the Group

Begin the faith-sharing process with these or similar words:
- Jesus recognized that the people of his time knew all about the concerns and difficulties of planting seeds and harvesting the yield, which is why the parable of the sower became such a powerful and memorable way to explain the various choices we have in connecting our faith with our life and the consequences of those choices.
- As you listen to the parable of the sower, think about the different opportunities you have had to live out your faith over the past few weeks and see if you can begin to identify the health of the seed you planted in the process.

Step 3: Proclamation of Scripture

Distribute pens or pencils and a copy of handout 5–A, "Scattered Seeds," to each participant. Provide the following directions:
- Look at the four types of ground on your handout and listen to the parable of the sower.

Invite the designated reader to proclaim Mark 4:3–9.

Step 4: Selection of Image and Meditation

Continue the handout activity with these directions:
- Look at the four quadrants of the field on your handout. Try to think of one recent situation or scenario from your life that illustrates what Jesus was saying about seeds falling on each of the four types of soil, and jot down a thought inside each of the quadrants. Then, ask yourself which quadrant seems to speak most powerfully to you at this moment and why.

Allow a few minutes for this reflection.

Step 5: Sharing Reflections

Invite the participants to begin sharing their reflections with these or similar words:

- ○ I now invite the prayer leader for each group to begin sharing the one quadrant that seemed to speak most powerfully to him or her as well as the meaning behind his or her choice. Please take turns sharing in your small groups, using the mutual invitation process.

Note: If the participants are unfamiliar with the mutual invitation process, take a minute to summarize the description on page 10 (see "Using the Mutual Invitation Process to Share Faith" in the introduction). Be sure to remind them of the option to pass.

Allow several minutes for this sharing.

Step 6: Conclusion and Closing Prayer

Conclude with these or similar words:

- ○ One of the things that allows us to remain rooted in good soil is our support of one another, especially through prayer. When we understand that we do not walk this journey of faith alone, it becomes easier to stay on the path that leads us to the good soil.
- ○ With that in mind, let us join hands and pray together a prayer that helps keep us centered in our faith, the Lord's Prayer.

Scattered Seeds

In each quadrant below, write about a situation in your life that illustrates what is happening to the seed that is being planted. Then look over the four scenarios and reflect on which one seems the most significant to you at this moment in time. Jot down your thoughts as to why it might be on your mind right now.

1. Seeds on the footpath: no-chance faith. It never had a chance, because the person was not paying attention, did not care, or turned away from faith altogether.

2. Seeds scattered on rocks: flash-in-the-pan faith. It has no roots. When tested, it fades away.

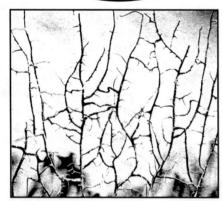

3. Seeds scattered among thorns: covered-up faith. It is smothered by other priorities, material possessions, fears, and indifference.

4. Seeds on good soil: good-news faith. God's word has been received, treasured, and nurtured and has grown so much that it has inspired others to have faith.